Chimes from the

Winds

of

Time

MAXINE LINDSEY PULLEY

D1438049

Fulton Books
Meadville, PA

Published by Fulton Books 2023

ISBN 979-8-88982-341-4 (paperback)
ISBN 979-8-89221-286-1 (hardcover)
ISBN 979-8-88982-342-1 (digital)

Printed in the United States of America

This book is not only about me and my journey but also about family and friends whom I have been close to in my early childhood, also about people in my life that I came to know along the way. Hard times but great times. Sad times but happy times. We were poor, but we didn't know because we were rich in love and faith.

I wrote this book for my children and the many generations to come. The joy and happiness as well as the struggles. Though it mostly did not seem like a struggle. Maybe they can learn something that will help them through their lives. I wrote it in love and respect of those who lived it and are gone on to another life. In honor of their memories, keeping their spirits alive in our hearts

Often in our life, our minds travel to another place and time; precious memories flood our soul. Back when times were so different. It takes me back to times when I can see my mother, father, or grandmother, working so pleasantly. So free and joyous that even though there was much hardship, it was often blotted out by their frame of minds. It is like working in my gardens, and suddenly a breeze flows through the trees, making the wind chimes play their music. And suddenly, my mind reminiscences to a time when it seemed as though nothing at all mattered. I was like a butterfly dancing from flower to flower. Only to be darting quickly away to avoid danger of some sort, which might be trying to overcome it. Then again, from bloom to bloom, upon branch to branch, and then fluttering away, returning to light upon the beautiful blossom swaying on the end of that branch. These are our memories. We are reminded of some memory that we quickly subconsciously run away from because it is so hurtful to remember that loved one, but if we bask in that memory, we can feel the joy of being there, sharing that part of our lives together.

This is what the *Chimes from the Winds of Time* is about—memories. Love of life and all the people in it. Our love for God and his love for us, the closeness of family and friends, and the endurances of times. It is also about the history of our nation and some of the people who helped make it so great. It is about a time that was and a time we wish for again. We didn't have much, but we had joy.

Whoever reads this book, I hope it triggers a chime from the winds of time for you that gives you a joyous moment, makes you smile, or laugh out loud. Maybe you will call a family member or a friend and reminisce. Maybe you will learn how to avoid the hurt by remembering the joy.

Some people are chosen to tell the stories, to love and cherish the stories, to keep them safe. Write them down and pass them on for those who do not have these precious memories. Some find it a privilege to share what they remember, hoping maybe that it might spark a memory that gives those without a reason to remember something to smile about and add blossoms and fragrance to their garden of life.

We are all on a journey through this world in the life we are given. We can choose to walk on through the paths of thorns, or we can stop along our thorny paths to take time to smell the roses.

Find some small glimpse of joy and beauty along the way that makes the path worth all the while.

Chapter 1

It was a long scorching summer already in the middle of July. The hot winds blew dust across the fields as the heat beat down upon the dry ground crusting and cracking the soil. Scorching the crops. The gardens were, too, being burned to a crisp. Everyone depended on their gardens to feed them until time for the gardens to produce the following year. They desperately needed a long rain, one that lasted a few days, a long soaking rain. One that would soak through the hard, dry ground to give those dry thirsty roots the moisture they were craving and needing to survive.

The women and the children that were old enough worked the gardens. Everyday hoeing and pulling weeds. Carrying water, picking, and preparing for the canning process. There were jars to be washed and wood to be chopped and split for the fires under those big washtubs full of water for washing and rinsing the jars, also to keep the fire in the cookstove going.

Most people had a screen porch with a cook table where the women prepared the food in the jars for the canning process. It was much too hot in the kitchen with the women trying to keep the woodstove at a proper even temperature for the water bath canner and the pressure cooker. The women always tried to can enough food to feed their families and those that fell upon hard times and might need a little help. They would dry fruit and vegetables and store vegetables in the cellar or smokehouse if they were blessed enough to live in a house with either of these. The men were all in the fields caring for the crops. The families depended upon the crops for the money their family needed to live on from crop till crop.

A lot of the food preservation had already been cared for, but there was still more to do. As with the crops in the fields.

Dwelling in a farmhouse near a hot dusty field was a family of six. The mother, father, and four children. Lee Lindsey, Adora Lindsey, and their children—Lona, age twelve; Dona, soon-to-be ten (she had a birthday coming up in September); Gerald, age eight, was to turn nine in August; and Nathaniel who was age two.

This morning, everything was all different in the little farmhouse. Company had been there all night. They had been up all night stirring around, in and out of the house to sit on the long porch. Talking among themselves. There were five more people—Willis Lindsey, Lee's father, and his wife, Mary Ida, Lee's stepmother. Van Swearingen, Adora's father, and her mother, Kate. Also Amy Eddings Cornett, Lee's aunt, his birth mother's sister. Aunt Amy was the family doctor. Although she was not a real doctor, she took care of everyone's medical needs. She had enough experience to be a doctor. She was a midwife to neighbors, friends, and family all over, anywhere she was needed.

Occasionally, you could hear Nathaniel whimper for his mother. He was easily soothed by Lona, who would rock him and sing to him until he dozed back off into a light sleep for a short time. Lona was a natural when it came to the care for the boy. She rocked him, walked around carrying him gently bouncing, whatever it took to get the job done. On this night and early morning, she had much help from Maw, who was also seeing to the two women in the bedroom as well as the men on the porch. Mary Ida was also trying to do all that she could for all of them. Maw always had a song or story or as many as it took.

The unusual appearance at the dinner table was uncomfortable for the children, yet the three older ones handled it very well. It was common for Adora to join Lee on the porch after the dinner table was cleared and the kitchen was cleaned. Tonight, it was Willis and Van who joined him and occasionally Ida and Kate but not Amy or Adora. The men talked about the war and updated each other on the most recent news of the soldiers that were family or friends. They talked about the crops and the heat and how everyone could use a good rain. Once in a while, one of the women would bring them a glass of sweet tea or a cup of coffee.

"Mom," Lee said to Ida, "keep that coffee pot on the stove if you will. I have a feeling that this is going to be a long night."

They rolled their cigarettes and stuffed their pipes. They smoked more than they usually did.

Kate would knock softly on the bedroom door with cool water for the women to drink and wash their faces. Sometimes, she would stay and give Amy a little break. The fan in the window of the bedroom blew in hot air.

"You children, go on to bed now," Lee said. "No reason for you to have to stay up. Some of us will wake you if something happens." He gave them all a hug and kiss as he tucked them in and told them a quick bedtime story as he always did.

The night wore on. The men would start pacing, and one of the women would bring them a cup of coffee and try to update them of the happens in the bedroom. They would settle down for a while. Occasionally, they could hear Adora's groans and become uneasy again. From the porch, they heard the groaning stop, a cry from an infant, and the three of them almost tripped over each other to get to the bedroom.

Amy called, "What time is it?" So she could record it on the birth certificate.

"Seven twenty-two a.m.," someone said.

Ida and Kate would not let them in the bedroom. After they had been given the news, the women let Lee go inside to his wife and new daughter.

The baby would not come but had to be saved if there was any way at all. The forceps were used to help pull the baby out of the birth canal before it suffocated. It was cleaned and wrapped and not a word was spoken before the tiny infant was handed to the mother. When she looked down at the face of the tiny little girl, she could not keep back the tears and the anger as her heart was breaking in two. The forceps had been applied directly across her face. Her tiny nose was crushed into her face and her forehead, and her ruby-red cheeks were caved in. The mother was hurting for her little girl but, at the same time, angry at Lee for not allowing her a doctor.

Maxine Elizabeth Lindsey, born in Ingleside, Arkansas, on Thursday, July 18, 1946, at 7:22 a.m.

Sometime in between these children, Adora had suffered a miscarriage, a set of twins that were still born and a child who only lived a few days because of heart problems. In those days, they referred to such a problem as a blue baby and thought there was nothing that could be done to save the child. The mother had begged her husband for a doctor to no avail. A doctor or hospital probably could have not saved the baby.

After losing the twins and a boy, James Rolland, the blue baby, she tried even harder to get a doctor's care with her pregnancies. However, he would not give in.

As the story goes, Willis had a major influence on Lee and was against the doctor.

She had three children since this child and finally got her doctor's care with them.

After the incident with her birth, Adora set her foot down and rebelled against Willis, and he was not allowed to be involved in any of their decisions ever again. Willis was known as a kind and gentle man and loved his family, but he was stubborn when it came to the way he believed.

There was another baby born in the family seventeen years later, on the same day, May 17, 1960. My sister Dona's third child. A baby boy. This baby's life was saved. He was born in a military hospital and had very well-trained doctors, who, after much travail, managed to save the baby.

Chapter 2

Story about Willis is debatable, but this is the way it goes according to Adora.

Since anyone did not know what to do for James Rolland, they couldn't stand seeing him suffer, so Willis did something to him to end his suffering. We don't know the whole of the story or if it is real. Adora always believed it to be true.

Lee and Willis would not let her see the baby, and she was very ill and could not force them to let her care for him. She always stuck to this story, and I believe her. Adora was not one to hold a grudge or invent such a story. It was not in her nature to be the kind of person together to dislike someone so much that she would invent a lie just to get to keep a grudge.

After I was grown, one of my great-aunts told a story which confirmed what Adora told after all. Grandmother, the sister of Lee's mother, Mary Elizabeth Eddings Lindsey, told me this story. I guess I am glad that I did not know these stories until after I was older.

Willis had an awful temper and was a very moody person. His mood could change in a heartbeat, and when it did, it brought along a temper fit which would cause him to take everything out on Mary.

The year was 1932. She was a tiny woman and very young when they married. She was from the Cherokee Indian tribe. She was fourteen years old when she had her first pregnancy. This child was my father, Alfred Lee Lindsey, and his twin, Albert. Unfortunately, Albert did not live.

Mary was thirty years old and had a houseful of young ones to care for. She had six children, ages from sixteen down to age of three. She had given birth already to eight children and was expecting again. Another set of twins—this was her third set. Willis came home from work, and something was not just right for him, so he went into one of his fits, and he beat Mary very badly. She went into labor and gave birth to the twins. Though she did not live to see them.

At the time, Lee was sixteen years old. He was very afraid of Willis. Willis would not let him cry over his mother. He said if Lee shed a tear, he would beat him to death too. Then he made Father build Mary's casket. He could barely hold back his emotions as he worked. The hurt, the fear, and anger. If Willis noticed the emotion breaking, he would yell at him and threaten him. He would not let anyone try to get contact to her family.

A few days later, Lee found a way to write a letter and get it into the mail to Mary's family and told them this story:

> Father and the rest of the children tried to care for the twins, but they didn't last long after they were born. My wild imagination wanders back to the story of James Rolland, and you can guess what I speculate happened to the twins.

Lee never spoke of this to anyone again as far as I know. About a year later, Willis married again. This was the grandmother I knew and loved. We had many happy visits with her. These stories do surprise me about Willis. He never seemed like the person in the story above. But children, being the innocent souls that they are and not knowing, often can sense things about people and shy away because of that, but this was not the case with Grandpa. He passed away when I was nine years old.

I don't know how he died, but I remember going to the funeral. The funeral service was held in the Jackson Funeral Home in Newport, Arkansas, and he was buried in the Sand Hill Cemetery just outside of Newport.

Chapter 3

Mother took it on herself to restore my face. She was so patient and did excellent work that today you cannot tell such a thing had happened. She pulled my nose up out of my face, stuffed my nose with rolled gauze, and propped my nose up on the sides with cotton and taped it, so it would not fall over. She pinched my cheeks and forehead up several times a day, trying to shape them. Each feeding would give Mother an opportunity to work with my face.

My mother was such an amazing person. There was not a spirit of giving up in her. She always said to us, "Don't say that you can't. You never know what you can do until you try, and you can do anything that you set your mind to if you try hard enough." I do believe that given the chance to try, she could have saved James Roland. I have always lived by that and have learned that there is a way to do what you want if you try hard enough to figure it out. I have tried to teach all my children and grandchildren the same thing and will continue with the future generations.

Later in years, I did have to have reconstructive surgery to some of the bones in my forehead. After a car wreck in my early forties, my head had hit the windshield twice and the x-rays showed the bones were crushed. What the surgeons found is that the bones had been crushed at birth, not even knowing the story. After I told them, they were amazed at what a remarkable job Mother had done with my face.

Though I never knew a thing about any of it, the next day was not much of a day for the adults who had been up all night. There were still chores and regular work for us to do, so everyone went back into action as nothing had happened. Willis and Mary Ida went back to their home in Cord, and Van went back to his and Kate's home in Shoffner. Willis gave Amy a ride to her home. Kate stayed to help for a few days.

There was company casually dropping in for the next few days. Most of the friends and neighbors knew what was up when the Lindsey family didn't show up for Wednesday night prayer meeting at their church.

My step grandmother was the one I knew as my grandmother. We loved her. We never knew that she wasn't dad's real mother until we were grown-ups. He never let it show. He always worried over her and was very respectful. He loved her just like she was his mother. She also had been married before and had a son around Dad's age. His name was Walter Woods. The two boys became remarkably close as if they were brothers.

Chapter 9

I never knew much about my mom's or dad's folks earlier in years before my grandparents. Oh, there were stories here and there from them and what my parents had been told or remembered from their youth. I loved my grandparents on both sides, the ones that I knew. I cherished the stories and the history.

My mother's father had passed away when I was three years old. The grandchildren called him Pa. I don't remember him. She told stories about him being a fur trader. During times of hardship, he ate snakes or polecats. He also taught music.

She had a brother—Essom was his name—and two half sisters, Lola and Nora Elizabeth. The sisters lived with their mother.

Mother told me a story about her mother, who we called Maw, about how she was cleaning the house. She was spring cleaning. Mother was tired of carrying water to boil and keeping the stove filled with wood. It was her job during this housecleaning process to keep the fire going and to have plenty of boiling water. Grandmother scrubbed the whole house from top to bottom. She washed the bed covers, quilts, and curtains. She took everything in the cupboards out and scrubbed down the cupboards. "The only way to keep away the chinch and diseases," she would say. Mother had been helping her when she found a nest of baby mice.

Being angry for having to work so hard and Maw keeping her going to the extreme, at least Mother thought, she thought she would have a little fun and get even with Maw. "Look, look, Momma, look what I found."

Maw screamed, "Throw those things out! Kill them, so they won't come back in this house!"

Mother laughed and pretended to throw them away.

Maw took to scrubbing that cupboard with boiling water and lye soap. While she was bent over with her head stuck inside the cupboard, Mother put the little mice down the neck of her dress. Maw banged her head on the shelf of the cupboard as she came out screaming. Struggling to get them out, she was screaming at Mother to help her, jumping and jiggling around the kitchen. It must have been a sight. Mother was laughing so hard she could not do a thing to help. Maw threw them out the door and spotted the rug beater leaning against the wall next to the door. Mother got the beating of her life. Maw stayed mad at her the rest of the day, making her work even harder.

Pa and Essom had been away. When they came home, Mother told them what happened, thinking she would get sympathy.

Pa said, "Now you know how Momma hates those mice. You shouldn't have done that." Then he said to Maw, "Now you didn't have to be so hard on her. You two are always playing tricks on each other."

Maw replied, "I guess you are right, but it gave me such a fright. Ugh, I can still feel them scrambling around on my back. It was such a horror that I felt them all the rest of the day, and every time that feeling got all stirred up, I got angry at Adora all over again."

The men could barely hold back, then out it came. They nearly rolled on the floor with laughter at what they imagined the day to have looked like at their house.

At first, Mother and Maw's feelings were hurt, and they were angry at them for laughing, then it hit them too. Even through dinner and the rest of the evening, one or the other of the men would burst out and then they all would laugh till they cried.

Kate was born on July 31, 1892, in Lake City, Tennessee. Her mother's name was Mattie Lunsford, born in Tunica, Mississippi, in August 1, 1859. She had been married to Allen Thrift before marrying Maw's father, Thomas Vance. Thomas was born in 1847 in Kentucky. They were married in 1868 and lived in Mississippi until moving to Bryant, Arkansas, in 1910. She had an older sister, Rosia Thrift, and two older brothers, Joseph and Allen Thrift. These were half siblings. She had an older brother, Thomas Vance; two older sisters, Leafy and Lidia Vance; a younger brother, William Vance; and younger sister, Maggie Vance. Kate married at the age of fourteen years to my grandfather, Damien Van Swearingen, who we called Pa. They moved to Bryant, Arkansas. The census being every ten years makes it hard to trace people and the exact times of the residency in between. Mother was born in 1912 in Stone County, Arkansas.

I never knew my grandfather Swearingen's real name until after I was a grown-up. A cousin told me the secret about his name. Her father, my uncle Essom, had told her. As the story goes, Paw never wanted to use his first name, Damien, because it reminded him of Satan, so he just dropped it. Mother or Maw never told us that. Perhaps he never told them. Maybe it was a well-guarded father-son thing.

Van was born in the year of 1874 in Macon County, Missouri, to Noah William Swearingen and Mary Elizabeth Craig. They had seven children. Van was the youngest. Noah was born in Tennessee, and Mary was born in Virginia. Noah was drafted into the military in August of 1863 to fight in the Civil War.

Maw never married again until she turned sixty-five years old. His name was Ezekiel Spradlin. She passed away at the age of seventy-seven in Newport, Arkansas. The same place that her mother, Mattie Vance, had passed away in 1915 at the age of sixty-three.

Our new grandfather, Zeke we called him, was like a grandfather to us. We loved him so very much. Some of us weren't born yet when we lost Paw, and the rest were too young to remember him.

Essom passed away when I was young also. I have some fond memories of him and his family. Mother's sisters both lived well into their nineties.

I wish that I had known my father's mother the way that I got to know Maw. We were remarkably close to Maw.

Chapter 5

O f course, I don't remember much about my life until after I turned two years old. And the memories are here and there, bits and pieces of places and happenings. These memories would begin in the year of sometime between January and July 1949.

I was born and lived the first few years of my life in a community called Ingleside, Arkansas, southwest of Newport. Many fond memories were made here at this area.

Dad, Mom and Maxine age two

I hardly remember moving into this house. What I remember most is this: In the front and other side were the roads. The road in front had a road turning from it, which ran down the side of our yard on both sides. Of that road grew a bean crop. It needed a lot of work inside and outside before we could live in it. Across the road in the front was a thicket and slew. Deep ditches ran between the roads and our yard in the front and side.

I remember Momma, Lona, and Dona cleaning and scrubbing and complaining about what a job it was because the house was so filthy. She told stories about how the house must have had a shoe salesman living in it. One of the bedrooms had been stacked full of shoes. A lot of them used. It smelled something awful. She had said, "We thought we would never get the smell out. She said they had to go over the house fumigating and sanitizing it. Then it had to have new wallpaper and floor coverings. What a job it had been to get that old wallpaper off the walls, so they could sterilize and spray the cracks between the boards for chinches, just in case they were breeding in there. They did the same thing to the floors after they stripped the old linoleum off. They replaced it with new linoleum and wallpaper, but before they did, they covered the boards with tar paper to help seal the cracks and help keep the cold air out. I have heard stories about how some people did not know to do all this. Sometimes they could not afford to, and the wind would blow through the cracks. Their house would be so cold, and at times, they would wake up to find ice or snow in their rooms. I felt so sorry for the people who suffered from the hunger and cold.

Chapter 6

There was a family who lived in a huge house on a hill. They had several children as our family did. The house had a porch all the way across the front of it and a picket fence around a very large yard. The boys, it seemed to me, were always whitewashing that fence. I remember my brother, Nathaniel, begging my mother to let him go help. He was only five at the time, but he loved whitewashing that fence. His face would carry a smile from ear to ear, and the other boys would be laughing as they worked. This family was one of many families that I remember in our community and in our church. Our families would get together for dinners, and my, what a spread of mouthwatering Southern cooking. The men and boys would fish, and the women and girls would be preparing a feast while they would be fishing. Then the fish were brought in, cleaned, and ready for the batter and then the frying pan. Oh my! I can still smell and taste that feast.

If we did not have company for Sunday dinner, we were at the house of friends. Several families would gather at each house for dinner after church. My mother was famous for her cakes. The young people favored her yellow cake with the hard fudge icings, and the older people favored her coconut cake. And there were her pies, fried pies, as well as the chocolate, lemon, and coconut meringue. She made the best yeast rolls. She knew how to cook. If she did not have an ingredient, she knew just what to substitute to make it taste the same. I do believe the whole congregation would gather somewhere every Sunday. I remember so well the women and older girls cooking and cleaning up. The men would be on the porch or smokehouse, talking; some of them caring for the young children, trying to keep them out of the kitchen. And the older children would play ball, kick the can, or hide-and-seek. When the women were free from the kitchen, the people would team up and pitch horseshoes.

Also, music, great music. My mother could play any instrument she touched and sing so beautifully. Mother's father had taught her to play the pipe organ when she was so small that her fingers could not reach the keys. He put empty shotgun shells on her fingers, so she could reach the keys. She often spoke about how he made her practice until her fingers hurt so badly that she thought they would break. She could barely stay awake; she would be so tired. Her mother would often feel sorry for her and would have let her quit, but her father would not give in. As she learned to play, she was glad that he kept the practice sessions up. Soon, she learned to play every instrument she could get a chance to play and picked it up quite rapidly. It was a natural for her.

Dad played the guitar and sang. Everyone in our family sang. Some of the other people in the church played various instruments and sang. There were always church singings, revivals, ice cream socials, and baptisms. People came from all over the state. My first name was chosen from a gospel singer in a group that Mother knew. The group became famous. I only wish that I could remember who they were.

It was at one of those church meetings that my father and mother had met. Soon after, they began courting and married. They both lived around Mountain View, Arkansas, at the time, in Stone County. Mother often talked about where she was from and how she missed living there. Mother was married before she married my dad. She was fourteen. He was from a community between Locust Grove and Mountain View. The marriage did not work out. They lived way out in the country. Quite away from anyone else. He would leave her alone and go drinking and partying. When he came home, he was mean to her. When my grandfather and uncle found out about it, they went and got her and took her home. Grandfather helped her get the marriage annulled. She was nineteen when she and Dad got married.

Chapter 7

Memories are so precious. Often reflecting upon an old memory of something that happened or a place we have been is like reading a short story. Sometimes bringing on a series of stories until it seems as though we are lost in a book, consumed, page after page, or intensely lost, lost in a movie.

The memories of my life started in the spring of 1949. I wasn't quite three years of age. Now I am not sure which activity came first.

We were at church service on a Sunday morning, and at the end of the service, the grown-ups were discussing upcoming events.

There had been a baptism in the planning. They were just waiting for the weather to get warm enough. I remember the grown-ups gathered around, talking about where it would be. It seemed as though they were having a difficult time finding a proper place. There was not a baptismal at the church, but most of the churches would use the river or a creek. Several places had been mentioned, but for some reason or another, they could not be used. I vaguely remember that the water was not deep enough in some of the places mentioned, even though they had used them before. Oh, but there was one place, and the only place with enough water for the preacher to dunk someone was a creek where there had been some sort of an accident which terribly disturbed the whole congregation. But there had to be a baptism, and it could not be done without water, so this was where it had been.

I really don't remember much about the accident that had happened there, except that someone's teenager had drowned, and it was not to be asked about or mentioned to anyone. Just forgotten.

I don't remember who was baptized or how many, but the thing that stands out in my mind was the alligators. The younger children were told, "Do not to get out in the water because of the alligators. They could swallow up a whole person. Stay near the bank in the shallow water and do not come out any further into the water. There could be an alligator hiding under the water and come up and get you." The older boys were to go down to the bend and watch for the alligators. The singing began, and the preacher spoke, and the dunking began.

Then suddenly, one of the boys screamed, "Alligator, alligator!"

The smaller children screamed and ran out of the water far up onto the bank, so we couldn't be eaten by the alligator.

I remember one of the men of the congregation said, "I will look," and went to the boys. He stayed there until the baptism was over. Then it was off to someone's house for a feast and fellowship.

Now I never knew if there were actually any alligators in that water or not. Maybe it was just a story that they told us, so we would obey and not wander off into deeper water. And most likely the boys that screamed out, "Alligator, alligator!" were just playing a prank as teenage boys often do.

Chapter 8

A wonderful feast and fellowship followed. Sometimes, I wonder, *Did the women ever get to rest with the cooking and the cleaning after all those gatherings? The caring for the children?* It appears everyone had several children. That made for ball teams and teams for the other games that we played. Oh, the ball games bring back memories too.

I was much too young to play ball, but I didn't know it. I think I always thought that I was older than I was. There were times that did cause trouble for me, and this day was one of those times. On this day, there were several families at our house for dinner after church. Dinner was over; the men were all gathered on the front porch deep in conversation about the weather, the crops, livestock, the Bible, whatever. It seemed like every time I went out there, they were on a different subject. The women were in the kitchen cleaning up the dishes and also discussing many things. All the children were out in the yard playing ball, except for two. One was the pastor's youngest son, and the other was me.

The pastor's son, Jackie, was two years older than me, same age as Nathaniel. Jackie had adopted me the day he first saw me as a tiny baby and had always thought that I was his baby sister. I never seemed to mind that so bad until this day. Nathaniel was my best friend, so I looked at Jackie as being the same. I never let anyone boss me. Nathaniel was always so kind and gentle with me that it never seemed like he was bossing. He probably just always let me have my way.

This day, Nathaniel was out playing with the older children, and I could not accept that. If he got to go, why couldn't I? I liked to play ball. So I cried and carried on and tried to sneak out. I did everything that I could to get out there to no avail. Back and forth, crying to Mom and then to Dad. The whole time, Jackie was trying to hang onto me and hug me and tell me no. I never liked to be held or kissed or hugged. I remember the pictures Mom had taken of me, shrinking up and squealing when Nathaniel tried to hug me. This day, Jackie would not leave me alone. I screamed and squealed and ran back and forth from one grown-up to another, trying to find someone who would make him leave me alone. "Oh, he is just trying to look out for you, or he loves you. Go tell your momma. Go tell your daddy. Go tell his mom. Go tell his daddy." I just got so aggravated at this that I bit him. He ran screaming and crying to his daddy, who was sitting right next to mine on the porch. Well, needless to say, I got a spanking. Then I ran crying back to our moms, who were both in the kitchen together just finishing up the dishes. They both got mad at the men. Jackie's mom went out to the front porch to look after Jackie to let him know that it served him right and that he should have left me alone like she told him to and to give the men a scolding. That boy had aggravated me all day long.

Jackie and I hated each other, and I didn't care. He left me alone from that day on.

Maxine age 3

Chapter 9

Time had rolled around for the fields to be prepared for planting. Whichever piece of equipment they used was pulled by a team of horses.

My father first broke up the garden and got it ready for Momma and the girls to do their planting. He had already broken it up earlier, so they could get the potatoes, cabbages, and other early crops planted. My favorite of these were the little English peas. Then he plowed the fields and got it ready for the harrowing. This was when he took Gerald to the fields with him to teach him. After a few times of working with him, showing him how to, he started leaving Gerald with the team in the fields when he would run errands. Every time Dad left him, the team became aggravated with Gerald and would not listen to him. Gerald was seven years older than me, which made him nine years of age turning ten in August.

Nathaniel and I were outside playing. It was a busy day for the household, so we were sent outside to play, so we would be out of the way. Mother and my two older sisters were hard at the house, cleaning and doing laundry.

I heard someone calling, "Help, help."

I said to Nate, "Listen, it is Gerald."

He made a dive for the door, yelling to my mom, "Gerald needs help! The horses are at it again."

Mom and the girls made a command for us to stay inside, but we could not handle the curiosity, so we ran out to the edge of the yard to watch as they took off for the field. We knew somewhat of what was going on; it had happened before. The horses had become rebellious to Gerald's commands and were trying to make a run for it. Mom headed for Gerald, and the girls headed for the horses. They got them under control, and the harrowing was off to what seemed like a good start. Mom and the girls came back to the house doing housework and laundry, and play was on its way again.

After a few minutes, it was déjà vu all over again. We could see Gerald far in the distance, lying on the harrow, and the horses making their getaway. The horses had become too contrary for Gerald to handle and had gotten out of control. His footing had slipped and gotten under the harrow. He had held onto the reins as the horses dragged him along, screaming for help as long as he could. Then he had to let go and let those stubborn horses have their way. This time, they could not catch the horses, and everyone came to the house disgusted with it all. My mother was angry at my dad for going off to run that errand and leaving Gerald in the field to do a man's work. This time, Gerald's ankle was swollen and was in bad shape. When Dad came back, he found Gerald and the team gone. He went to the house to check on Gerald and took off to find the horses in a pen at the neighbor's. After he got them back, he worked until it was so dark he couldn't see. Mom was still upset at him.

There were many young boys that worked at such task around the farm. It was different with Gerald. Dad didn't want to let anything hold Gerald back from feeling like he could do anything the other boys at his age did. But Mom was more protective and worrisome over him.

It had been the time of the polio epidemic that affected so many children, and Gerald had been one of them. A lot of children were left handicapped if they even lived. Gerald was one of the more fortunate children, even though he did not walk until he was four years old and left with a defected hip bone.

He told me a story about being left on a quilt at the end of the field or maybe the garden; he did not remember which. He just remembered being left there on a pallet while the family was in the field or garden working. There he was, on the quilt and could not move, when out of nowhere, he saw a horse running full speed right at him, and he could not get out of its path. Everyone left their task to try to reach Gerald before the horse did but could not run fast enough. When the horse saw the child, he jumped right over the top of child and quilt. He was paralyzed from the waist down and could not move out of the way. The beast knew and did whatever it took to keep from harming the child.

It is hard to believe that after a scare like that, in just a few years later, the boy would oversee the giant beast working them in the fields. Daddy didn't put Gerald back out there again. When he needed help, Mom or one of the girls would go help him.

It did not seem like it was very long at all until the corn had grown a huge wall of tall corn all around the back and side of our house. In the back, behind the wall of corn, and on creek bank grew a narrow line of trees from which Dad cut our firewood for the cookstove and heating stove we used in the winter.

Chapter 10

I remember well the day my sister, Joyce, was born on July 12, 1949. It had rained and rained hard. From the things that I remember, it was much needed. The hard rain quickly filled the ditches by our house, which were full of muddy water.

As soon as the rain stopped, Nathaniel and I had ran off to play in the water. Daddy walked down the road by our house to look at the water in the fields and let us tag along. He let us play in the water-filled ditches. Later when we returned to the house, we begged him to let us go back and play more. Mother was worried about it, but I remember my dad say for her to let us, that everything would be all right. Lona and Dona took care of Nathaniel and I while they were gone.

The next memory that I have is my dad coming to find us playing in that muddy water and telling us that we had a little sister, and if we would go to the house and get cleaned up, we could go back to the hospital with him to see her. Needless to say, we hurried out of the water as fast as we could. The girls already had water warmed on the stove for our baths. It didn't take them long to bathe us and get us dressed. They were just as anxious to go to the hospital to see Momma and the new baby. Joyce Ruth Lindsey was her name.

We wanted to run down the halls. We were both so anxious to see our baby sister.

"Now, now, we must walk quietly and talk quietly," Dad told us. "There are sick people in here. They need to rest."

We went directly to the nursery, where Dad pointed her out to us and lifted us to the window for a better view "Oh, oh" was about all we could say. Then it was time and time again, "When will we take her home?" and "Can I hold her?" He had a hard time pulling us away from the nursery window for a visit with Momma. There she was, when we walked in the door, sitting up on the bed, waiting for us with a big smile and her face all aglow, so eager to see us. And we all shared our excitement over the baby girl.

Chapter 11

A well-dreaded news, even for the younger children. It was in the fall of the year; Daddy had found a new job with another farmer, and we had to move to a new farmhouse. We needed a larger house and barnyard too, and this one had all that and more. That didn't seem so bad after all.

Momma and Daddy had already told the older children—Lona, Dona, and Gerald—at the breakfast table. Later in the day, she had told Nathaniel and I that we were moving into a different house, and she needed all the help she could get to get everything ready to be moved. We could help a lot if we just played in the yard.

Every time we went into the house, they would be busy packing. Boxes everywhere. Some things were bundled up in sheets, like the linens and some of the clothes. The dishes were packed up in washtubs.

Dad was busy getting the barnyard animals ready and all the things out of the shed—ploughs, tools, bridles, saddles, and so on. He made several trips to the other house before he was ready for the boxes and then the furniture. He took everything he could take for the day, and they just kept what we would need for the night and next morning. We got up very early and took the last load. It was exciting for Nathaniel and me.

Mom was so glad not to have to do a lot to the new house as she did in the old one. Though you can be sure that she went over it with a fine-tooth comb as far as the cleaning went, but it didn't have to have a makeover like the one we were moving out of. A new home was like a new beginning. It wasn't a new house, just a different one, but it was new to us and so many things more to explore. I loved it.

It was time for Dad to harvest his peanuts and popcorn. We found him in the peanut patch. The family that lived here before had planted the popcorn and peanuts and let Dad harvest them since they couldn't come back to do it. Dad was so pleased because he loved popcorn and peanuts. We all did. As a family, we spent many nights all gathered in the living room waiting for the peanuts to be roasted and the popcorn to be popped. That was Daddy's duty; he thought no one could do it as good as him, and he had to do it. But he would say he perfected a way to get them just right. He would always say, "Now you got to do it like this... It has to be done just this way." We would get anxious for them to be ready to eat at times. He would say, "You got to be patient. It takes time to do it just right."

My, how we loved to help. I know that we weren't a lot of help at our young age. My dad was patient with us trying to show us just what to do, and we had so much fun with it. He pulled the plant up and shook off most of the dirt, then he handed us each a plant and said, "It is easy, just shake like this," then he had us lay them all in a pile. After a few plants were pulled, he said, "Now we have to pull the peanuts off."

Nate and I loved to play farm. We took nails that we found lying around the barn and put them in rows around our farm to use for fence post. Then we plowed our fields and made them ready to plant. We took narrow leaves and stuck them down in the sandy soil for corn and twigs, with small leaves for other plants. We made our houses and other buildings out of twigs and popsicle sticks. We played for hours like this.

Chapter 12

The White River lies nearby, and we were warned to never go there, and as far as I can remember, we never ventured that way unless we were with one of the grown-ups. Sometimes, they would take us fishing. They would take along a picnic lunch. What a delight. I can still hear my dad sing the song about the ten little Indians and how one of them didn't get back into the canoe. I was full of questions about this song, and Dad would patiently try to answer each one to my satisfaction. I think he tried to use that song and that part of one not getting back in the canoe to make us think that the little Indian had drowned because they were playing in the canoe without permission and were not old enough to know how to handle the situation, to keep us from getting too close to the water, and it worked very well.

Another reason we never went toward the river was because we had to go past the haunted graveyard. Now I never saw a grave. I often asked where the graves were. Apparently, as the story was told to us, there was a very mean man buried there, and often you could hear him moaning. Sometimes, he would let people pass, but it depended on what mood his ghost was in. We were afraid that if we tried to sneak by him, that he would know the truth and send his ghost out to get us. One thing was as bad as another. We were good children and hardly ever got in the slight trouble.

Once Lona and Dona took Nate and I there. No, they were not twins; they were born eighteen months apart, and Gerald, my oldest brother, was twenty-three months younger than Dona. Then five years later was Nate. Mom had lost a set of twins and James Rolland during those five years.

Back to the trip to the cemetery… The older three were hunting for mussel shells; they took them and ground them up for the chickens. The oyster shells provide a good source of protein for chickens. This is why we get a good source of protein from eggs. Mom was always studying to try to find better ways to provide us with the necessities to stay healthy. The shells had to be just perfect. This is different than grit; chickens need grit also, which they get in different ways, but one way is ground-up eggshells. They need the grit to help their gizzards to be able to grind up their food and make it easier to take the good out of their food and pass the waste out. So much to learn when you live on a farm. Mom and Dad were very particular when it came to taking care of the animals. They had to have healthy animals to be able to produce what they needed for raising healthy kids.

Nate and I begged to come along. I could never understand what these mussel shells were doing in the cemetery and could not get a satisfactory answer. I spoke my disbelief that it really was a cemetery at all, and there was not even a mean man. That it was just a story.

As I was speaking, I picked up what I thought was as an exceptionally large mussel shell, and Gerald grabbed it from my hand and said, "Oh, that is someone's jawbone." He began to bury it.

I asked him, "What are you doing?"

He replied, "I must bury it, so whoever it belonged to will not come looking for it."

I answered in disbelief, "That is just an old shell and don't belong to anyone."

He said, "Probably it belonged to someone that had walked through the cemetery without the permission of the ghost of that mean man who was buried here."

"What is his name?' I asked.

He made up some name of the person he thought that it was. I did not believe that story either.

So Dona said, "We better go. I think we have got him upset. Listen, he is beginning to moan."

All I heard was the wind blowing through the trees.

At three, I had already developed a mind of my own and was very hard to be persuaded. I had a lot of questions and did not want just any answer. It had to be what I thought was a reasonable answer, or I would not accept it.

Chapter 13

Now there was Mom, Dad, and six children. At our dinner table, there were four chairs and a bench. The younger children sat on the bench. Mom, Dad, Lona, Dona had the chairs. If Maw happened to be there, she took a chair and four were on the bench, all lined up in a row. Older ones to both outside spaces on the bench—Dona at one end, Gerald at the other—Nathaniel and I in the middle. Joyce would sit on someone's lap.

How I loved the tasty food. As I said before, my mom was quite a cook and so were my sisters. There were always pigs and chickens in our home. There would also be canned vegetables from the garden or food that they stored in the cellar. Also canned and dried fruit. Mom used the dried fruit for her delicious fried pies. She could turn out a great chocolate fried pie too.

Dad was a hunter, so often we had wild game or fish on the table, as well as pork or chicken, and most of the time rabbit. Dad raised tame rabbits as well as hunted them. Nathaniel and I learned very young how to care for the smaller animals, like the rabbits and chickens. We also learned at an early age how to make a rabbit snare to keep them out of the garden.

Nathaniel and Maxine ages three and five

We had some great times sitting around the woodstove in our living room. After the work was done and dinner was over, while Mom and the girls cleaned the kitchen, Dad and the boys brought in wood for the heating stove to last through the night, and the cookstove for breakfast the next morning was all filled and ready to stick a match to. Momma's wood cookstove had a water reservoir on the side of it. She kept it filled with water, so we would have hot water for bathing. After supper was cooked, she had the boys carry in lots of water. They carried it in from the well out behind the back porch. There was a very deep hole that had water in it all the time from a spring bubbling up out of the ground way down deep. It had a bucket on a chain running across a pulley attached to a pole at the top of the little shelter around the well. The bucket looked like a long tube. The boys would let the bucket down until it bubbled, which meant it was full of water. I loved to watch them draw the water. They emptied the water from the well bucket into a water bucket then carried it into the house.

They usually had a foot tub also. Mom would fill the dishpans and put them on the stove. She would also have a teakettle and foot tub on the stove too. While the wood from the cooking burned down into red-hot coals and then turn to ashes, she would be able to heat enough water for cleaning the kitchen and for our bathing. First, it would be the little children. Mom used a foot tub for the smaller ones and the wash tub for the older children, and there we bathed in the kitchen while it was still warm from cooking supper. After the children, the adults would take their turn bathing in the washtub. Daddy often complained about the washtub. He wanted a bathtub. He had one, but it had gotten left behind at one of the moves. Sometimes, they had no way of moving everything they had accumulated, so they had to pick and choose what had to be left behind.

We all gathered into the living room, often playing games, singing, and eating Dad's fresh popcorn and fresh roasted peanuts. Dad always had stories to tell. Mom and the two girls were always doing some sort of needlework as they sang along and laughed often, even joining in the games. Often Maw would be at our house for a few days. Sometimes, even Maw would have a story to tell.

One among the many was a story about her grandparents, her mother's parents—Augustine Lunsford and Caroline Jane Glasscock Lunsford. They lived along with their four children—JR Davis and Harriet Davis, Margaret often called Mattie, and Mary Louisa—in a port house on the Mississippi River. This house was named the Lunsford House. It was used not only to receive and ship cargo but as hotel. Passengers would sometimes stay over. Caroline cooked and served meals to the passengers. She also baked pies, cakes, and other baked goods and sold them to women around the city. JR would deliver the baked goods to the customers.

The Union Navy came up on a ship and took over the port house. They shot their cannon into the house, leaving bullet holes all in the walls and took it over.

Augustus Lunsford, her grandfather, was in the army at the time and was left blind in a hospital in Alabama. He had been shot in the head. His hospital was like many of the hospitals, the wounded soldiers were in a home turned into a place to care for the wounded by the families that lived there. After several months, he was able to return to the military and was later killed.

Chapter 14

Among all the stories... Daddy's mother was Cherokee Indian. She had taught him to speak different language from some of the different tribes. He would often speak or sing a little in one of those language, and we would beg him to teach us to count and speak some of the language. Sometimes when we were gathered around the stove, he would teach us a song or to count in the Indian language.

This was also where Dad read the Bible and explained the meaning of what he read. Answering out questions and sometimes using a happening of the day for an example. When one of us had been naughty, he might use it as an example. But never in a way to make us feel humiliated or intimidate. He might say something like, "Does that sound like something one of you might have done today?" Someone would call a name. Most usually, each of us whose name was mentioned would say, "That wasn't me." Different ones would say, "Oh, yes, it was." If we got puffed up at being blamed, it didn't last long.

Sometimes, we would all be working, and it was like we didn't even realize it. We shelled peas or ground corn for corn bread or cracked corn for chicken feed. Dad had a small table set up with a grinder on it, so we could sit there and use it. They also used it to make the sausage, but it would be moved back to the kitchen for that task. All the children were very anxious to help, and Mom or Dad would always be willing to let us try. One of us would turn the handle and grind the corn until we were tired, then the other would take a turn. We would be ready and willing for our next turn. Work never seemed like work when the whole family was there laughing at someone's joke with a story to tell or a song to sing. We fell asleep quickly when tucked in bed at night and slept soundly with a peaceful ending to our day.

Mother was extraordinarily talented. She could look at a picture of a garment and cut the material out and sew it right up without having to go buy a pattern. It didn't matter if it was a shirt, pants, skirt, blouse, a dress, or sleepwear. Mother would sing and laugh with the rest of us as she made that old pedal sewing machine sing too. I can remember the flour and sugar came in sacks made from pretty cotton material. We were not the only children wearing flour sack or sugar sack clothes.

But that was not the only thing Mother could make. She made her own curtains, bedspreads, coverings for the couch and chairs, pillows, or whatever else was needed in the home. But then almost all the women and girls during that time were talented in many ways. Men as well as women were taught from generations back to be as self-sufficient as possible. They were taught to think ahead and find a way to put their minds to work to figure out the answer for any hang-up that occurred. Never give up; where there is a will there is a way. Try to do a great job because the Lord wants you to always strive to do your best. It brings glory to his name.

I can remember my dad working very carefully to put a new sole on someone's shoes or mending some sort of leather used in his farming, such as a harness or reins for his horses. My father knew how to quilt and sew clothes as well as some women. I have watched him mend his jacket or pants or sew a button or snap on a garment for one of the children. He would cut a new piece of leather for a shoe and sew it on. It would look like it was new.

Chapter 15

Then came the snow, and what fun we had in that beautiful white fluff. Across the road was an embankment, and the older children along with neighbor children had such fun sliding down that embankment on pieces of cardboard. Then they had snowball fights. Nate and I were not allowed to go out. Soon, Nate begged long enough that he got to go. The older children promised to take care to watch out for him. I cried and begged, and every time they came in to warm up by the stove, I persisted even more until finally they promised to take care of me if Mom would let me out for a while.

We climbed up the embankment to slide back down again time after time just as the older children did. Oh, what fun we had until while climbing up. The hill was becoming hard to climb for Nathaniel and me. It was getting slippery with solid ice, instead of the fluffy white snow. I slipped several times. Nate begged me to go inside before I got hurt, but I would not; I was having too much fun. And then I slipped several times trying to go back up that last time and almost gave up, but no, I wanted to have a little more fun. Then I lost my footing and slipped, busted my chin open from one side to the other underneath. Mom scolded the other children for not watching out for me more. Then she hugged them and apologized before dismissing them to go back out and told them that she was really upset with herself for letting me go out in the first place. They begged her not to feel bad at herself. I could tell that they wanted to be angry. After a time of crying and begging, she gave in. They all felt sorry for me and had promised to watch out for me, but I was ruining their fun. They must have really loved me because they couldn't let themselves keep those feelings against me.

They ran back out to play with friends, and I was satisfied inside after that. I was happy for the chance of fun that I had while I got out. But for now, the warm spot that I shared with Joyce, sitting on the quilt behind that woodstove, felt mighty good to me.

Christmas was coming soon. Mom let us pick our presents out of a mail-order catalog, although Dad thought they might carry those toys at the dry goods store, where they bought their supplies from. Mom was afraid they would be out closer to Christmas, and she did not want to risk it. I don't know if they had them at the store or came mail order; all I remember is that we got them along with the apples and oranges, crème drops, and hard candy that we got every Christmas.

We always had a lot of excitement getting ready for our Christmas. We sometimes got to go with Daddy to find the tree if the weather was good, snow was okay and fun, if it was not very deep but not cold rain or ice, and only if we didn't have a cold or something.

Mother had her ornaments and garland that she carefully wrapped and stored away, but we strung berries and popcorn and made ornaments out of foil. Daddy would help us thread our needles and show us how to push the needle through in a way as to not break the popcorn cornel or split the berry. We each made our own strings of popcorn and berries. He would lead us in different Christmas songs. He knew all of them. He would usually start off with "Up on the house top, good Saint Nick..." We would sing each one over a few times then "Rudolf, the Red-Nosed Reindeer" and several more, then he would end with "Santa Claus is Coming to Town." He wanted us to think about that one. The thought that Santa Claus was watching us and could see if we were naughty made us think a lot; we didn't want him to think we were naughty. He only brings gifts to boys and girls that were good. We tried hard to be very sweet and helpful to each other.

Lona and Dona liked to find the sycamore trees and gather the spiky seedballs that fell from it. They wrapped the balls in foil to make ornaments. They loved working with those. Mom made sugar cookies in the shape of angels, stars, bells, and Santa Claus, and we hung those on the tree too. It took several nights' worth of work, but we loved it. We sang Christmas carols and told our favorite Christmas stories while working. Then the last of all, when the day came that all the decorations were made and put on the tree, then the icicles were hung on the tree—those long streams of shiny silver—and someone would hang on the popcorn. The string of berries draped over the windows and doorways. And there you would have it.

We would have plenty of time to make candies, cookies, and popcorn balls. The homemade fudge was so delicious. My favorite though was the divinity. Mom made candied fruit slices and candied watermelon rind.

This time of the year was a very busy time of the year. Different family members would try to sneak around for a private place and spare time to make gifts for others. Maybe a set of dresser scarfs, perhaps a new apron, or a tablecloth, place mats and napkins to match, pot holders and dish towers to match. One of the men may have wanted a wool shirt or scarf, maybe a new vest.

Then the gathering and wrapping the presents for different family members and friends would be next. Simple but thoughtfully selected. Something that each one needed and would be pleasantly grateful for. A pair of warm wool socks, warm gloves, wool scarf, hairbrushes and handheld mirrors, the floral hankies with lace trim, stockings, perfume or lotion while the men liked hats, gloves, a warm pair of wool socks or scarf, a pocketknife, or a tool. Maybe some, a new pair of long underwear. Everything was wrapped and no one knew for sure what they were getting.

The night we waited for was here. The night before Christmas Day. We had all worked hard to help Mom get ready for that day, cleaning and baking. She needed a lot of water and firewood for the cookstove.

The dusk of the day had turned to the black dark of the night, yet the moon came, and the stars lit the darkness just perfectly reflecting their light down upon the fallen snow.

Dad tucked us into bed and talked to us about going to sleep, so Santa could come. "Now go to sleep," he said. "You don't want to hold Santa up by not going on to sleep. That wouldn't be fair to the other children who are waiting for him."

We tucked in our excitement just as he had tucked us in and let the sleep come. Our sleepy eyes closed, and the sleep took over.

"What? Morning light, yes!"

I heard voices from the kitchen.

"We could get out of bed. Nathaniel, Joyce, wake up. Let's go see if Santa came."

Up out of the bed and through the house, we ran, squealing with excitement, "Mom, Dad, did he come? Did he?"

"Let's go see."

One of us would go look.

And yes, there was Nathaniel's gun that he wanted, and Joyce's, and my doll that we had picked out in the catalog.

Chapter 16

All during the day, just as during the whole season, there were visits from family, friends, and neighbors. It was a beautiful and exciting time. Work came to a halt during the Christmas season and into late January, except for the daily chores of caring for the farm animals and keeping the kindling cut for the cookstove and heating stove. Also, we would bring up the wood on to the porch to keep both stoves going. The wood for the cookstove went on the back porch, and the wood for the heating stove went on the front porch. They also had to keep the water carried from the spring to the house. And for the animals that were in pens. If they could go to the pond and it had ice, they had to break the ice, so they could get water. Of course, even in the barnyard and pens, the water had to be checked to see if it had been frozen. Even though there was no work in the fields, there was still plenty to do around the farm.

Of course, as with all women, their work never stops. Mom had Dad move the washer onto the back porch. He had covered the screen to keep it warmer for them. The porch was cleaned off and scrubbed up; the cover taken off the screen in the spring through the summer and used for a place for the dining room table. We ate our meals out there. It was so much cooler than inside, where the kitchen and dining area was all heated up from the cooking.

The women did the washing, mending, ironing, as well as everyday cooking, cleaning, and caring for the children. Mom, like many women, did not always have a washing machine; there was a time when she as well as other women used a rubboard in a tub of water to rub the clothes clean. They made their laundry soap just like all the other soap that was used.

At night as we gathered around the living room as a family, we listened to more stories about times of the past. Momma liked to talk about her ancestors on the Swearingen side of the family. She had a grandfather, several generations back, who was a captain in the army. He was a friend of Gen. George Washington.

George Washington was out one day, touring the countryside to see how things were going for the people. He stopped to visit Grandfather, Capt. Van Swearingen, at grandfather's pub. He gave Captain Van his sword as a token of their friendship. That sword hung over Captain Van's fireplace mantle until his house, which by this time was occupied by one of his sons, was overcome and burned by soldiers during the Civil War. His son rebuilt the house but unfortunately was unable to save the sword.

Wintertime was a great cold and flu season. When one of the children got sick, it usually went around to each one. The only medicine I ever remember Mom or Dad, even Maw, used was hot lemonade with one Bayer aspirin for the children and two aspirin for adults. That broke the fever and stopped that flu in its tracks. No matter how achy, how high the fever was, or how runny that nose was, a dose of that helped you fall asleep for a couple hours, and when you woke up, you were so much better. If we had a cough and congestion, they rubbed Vicks salve on our chest, under our nose, and between our shoulders and kept a kettle of steaming water on the stove. We were never very sick for long. Sometimes, they used warm mustard. They would put it on a cloth and place one on your chest and between your shoulder blades. This was great for bronchitis. I have heard them talk about using mustard for almost all illnesses. Everyone almost always had catnip tea for an upset stomach. Maw rubbed it on her legs to take away the pain of her arthritis.

As soon as everyone was better, we were able to pitch in to give the house a thorough cleaning to get the air of the illness out and get freshness in.

Chapter 17

S pring was here, and it was time to get the ground ready for the planting. Birds were singing in the trees, and the squirrels were hopping from branch to branch. We were beginning to see the signs of new birth—baby rabbits, baby chicks, and baby ducks waddling around after their mommies.

The garden was already planted with the early crops. The fields were being prepared for planting. Animals were being moved from their winter homes to the spring and summer homes. Pens and stalls were being cleaned, and fresh straw was put down. Some of the hens were already sitting on their eggs as were the other fowl. The other animals—horses, cattle, pigs, and rabbits—were soon to deliver their little ones. I loved this time of the year. A true sign that spring is in full bloom as well were the beautiful blooms and buds on flower bushes and trees. Also the little ones springing forth from the barnyard animals.

Momma followed Maw's tradition every fall and spring. The cleaning was on. The women took the mattress outside to sun. Sometimes Dad would help if he happened to come by at the time. He saw one of them hard at beating the mattress and rugs with a long tool that they called a rug beater. To me it resembled a huge snowshoe. The furniture was all cleaned the same way. It was moved out to the porch and given a good beating. The bed frames were moved and disinfected; sometimes they received a fresh coat of paint. Floors were swept and scrubbed while the beds were out. Curtains and windows were washed. The whole house from top to bottom was cleaned, and not a piece of furniture, window, or wall was left uncleaned. Fresh paint was applied where needed. Maybe they would put up fresh wallpaper. Everyone in the house worked.

We woke up one morning to my mother buzzing around like crazy. "Okay, now let's get these children up and dressed and breakfast over and the housework done as quickly as we can. I want the front porch cleaned too. Come on, everyone, now let us get at it!"

What in the world was all the excitement all about? So much excitement that I hadn't even noticed that Dad was not there until he came up in the yard.

"Well, where is he at?" Mom asked.

"He said that he can't come today. He is shorthanded in the store. He will come tomorrow for sure."

Mom was so disappointed, and everyone seemed to be, and all that rushing around was for nothing.

The next morning came and the same rushing around. Along about midmorning, a delivery truck pulled up in the front yard and backed right up to the porch to unload Mom's first Maytag. She would never again have to rub clothes clean on that rubbing board. My, was she happy. The whole family was happy and gathered so close to see until she could barely get to the accessories inside the tub. Guess what was next. Dirty laundry flying around being sorted and tubs for the rinse water were being set up. The whole family was involved with the laundry that day. Listening to the new washing machine working was music to our ears.

Mom had Dad build her a large wooden box to set on the porch to keep the dirty laundry in during the summer. There was no air-conditioning for us. Just an oscillating fan. Mom said the laundry would smell up the house.

One day, we were doing laundry outside. Mom had already done several loads and was near the last of the wash when I looked back at the porch for some unknown reason, and there was an exceptionally large black snake crawling out of the box.

I tugged on Mom's dress, and she responded, "Maxine, what is it? [Meaning, what do you want?]"

I was much frightened as I replied, "Look, Mom, what is that coming out of the laundry box?"

"Oh my!" Mother said.

As she headed for the porch, Gerald and Nathaniel were already there. Lona and Dona followed.

I wonder how long that thing has been in there.

I was so amazed that she was not afraid at all.

She said, "One of us must have left the lid open. We will have to be more careful about to see that it is closed in the future." Then she chased the snake off and took the rest of the laundry out to see if there were more snakes in there.

She made Dad fix the box so that it would close so tightly that nothing could crawl in. She did not kill the snake but explained to us the difference between bad and good snakes. Now to me, none of them were good. She, knowing this thought, showed us the design of the heads and how to tell by the shape which ones were poisonous. She said while the black snakes, like the one that we had just seen, were not poisonous, they might make us sick if we were bitten, and they would eat the eggs if allowed to get into the chicken house where the nests were; they also ate baby chickens and ducks, though they do eat rats and mice and other pests that were harmful to us. The rats would eat the root crops and corn stored for winter. They would also get into our house and eat our food and clothes. If they were allowed to do this, they would build nests in our clothes and have babies that would get loose in our house.

I had found those baby mice in the barn. They were so pink and cute. Nathaniel and I had played with them, carried them around, ripped up in pieces of cloth, called them our pets until one day, Mom caught us. She took them and got rid of them and told us not to play with them again.

I could not understand this story that she had told us of how that ugly snake could be of help to us by destroying those small cute pink pets; how can that be right? We hated all the snakes after that.

Chapter 18

What now? All the rustling around again. Everyone, up, get dressed, make your bed, come to breakfast, clean the kitchen… Oh my, what now?

She was waiting for her Singer sewing machine to be delivered. I can still see her face, the excitement that was on it. Just as when she waited on the delivery of that Maytag washing machine, I can still see her. Waiting patiently, smiling, and singing, just like she did as she sat and pedaled that machine. She was singing as she sewed. Mom was always happy even when she worked. Always singing, smiling, and laughing.

Mom had made a trip to the store in Shoffner. They had a lot of pretty spring materials in stock. I was thrilled when she came home with material to make me a new dress and a pair of black patent shoes to go with it. I loved the shoes.

As we gathered around the living room at night, there she sat pedaling that machine and humming songs. Dad would look over at her and smile as he kept us entertained by telling us stories about the ancestors. We loved to listen.

One of our favorite things to hear was about how our ancestor had come over from other countries on a large ship. One of our grandmothers had come over on a ship by herself with nine children. Her name was Anna Marie Vincent. The whole family was waiting on the ship to arrive when her husband become very sick and passed away. She and the children settled in Virginia. Later on, they moved to Kentucky. They lived on a huge mountain. As the children grew up and built their own homes, they too built it on the mountain. There were homes all up the mountain with just a trail leading to the top. As the families at the bottom saw a stranger coming on the trail, they would whistle to let the next then the next family know that someone was coming, and on it would go whistling up the mountain. Because of this, the mountain was named Whistling Mountain.

During the times of the year when we would dig our potatoes out of the garden, Dad would always like to talk about the potato famine that happened to some of his ancestors from Ireland.

Chapter 19

We didn't have a car at this time; we rode in the wagon led by a team of horses everywhere we went.

The three older children walked through the fields to meet the school bus in the morning. They had to walk so far that in the fall and winter months, it was dark when they left to catch the school bus, and it would be dark when they returned home.

We rode in a wagon pulled by a team of horses to church, through a pasture, dodging some of the cows because they were too stubborn to move out of the way. The only roads were gravel, and some were like paths. Except in the city.

On Sundays and Wednesdays, we rode to church. Many times neighbors would ride with us. At this time, we went to a church in a tent. I loved the singings, the revivals, and the special prayer meetings. All the people we knew had the same kind of life. There were those who were better off and some who were not as well off, but everyone helped each other. I never knew any person who had what we knew as a rich life, who was not very generous with those who were not as fortunate.

After church, the pastor had called a meeting. It seemed like they were always holding a meeting after church. This time, he wanted to talk to them about raising money for the church. Since everyone was having such a hard time just trying to take care of their families, there wasn't much money in the offering. No one could afford to give any extra. Pastor George wanted to talk about some sort of fund raising to get some money for the repairs and to get the piano tuned. All women were very talented with their needlework and using what scraps they had left over in their sewing boxes to create beautiful crafts.

They often held quilting bees for such occasion, and people would buy chances for the quilts. Among other things created from their scrap material would be food warmers; they could put the food in this when taking it to a church social of family gathering to keep their food warm. They also made cotton dishcloths, tablecloths, pot holders, and aprons. All with beautiful needle work stitched on them. They made pies, cakes, cookies, and candies. All for display to be sold. At the event, the single women would bring a dinner. It should be a secret as to who made the dinner. It was to be auctioned. Each buyer of a dinner is to eat that meal with the lady that made it. Most of the time, the lady would let her boyfriend know which dinner had his favorite food, so he would know that she had made it. If another man would auction on it, either because he loved that food or he was interested in the lady, it would raise quite a bid before one would give up.

I heard Dad say that Mr. Aheart had requested for anyone that could give him a hand; he sure would appreciate the help mending the roof on his barn. The recent storm that had come through the area blew up giant trees by the roads and tossed them around. It had torn part of the roof off his barn. Most of the men agreed to help him, all that were able.

The women agreed and set a date for their function and picked a couple of ladies to organize the times of their meets and who was volunteering their house at which time for their meet. Another pair of ladies would keep track of what was being made and how much. They chose someone else to find a suitable place for their function. There were no phones at this time, so everything had to be done by mail or word of mouth. If a person needed to spread the word to someone, just tell the mailman, the school bus driver, your husband, or anyone you knew that would be going the way of the person you wanted the word spread to. That got the job done.

Money was as scarce as it was for people to have on hand; the fundraiser did not acquire enough money that was needed for the church. The next possibility was a tent. Mr. Aheart had donated some land for the tent and for people to park their teams, or if some was fortunate enough, they could have a space for their automobile. This seemed to be great for all.

The next thing I remember was going to church in a huge tent. All the men had gotten together to set up the tent. It had wooden floors and a large woodstove in the front. They had the pulpit set up with the altar benches on both sides. There were even places for class-rooms divided off with canvas curtains. The adults and young adults had their classes on separate sides of the congregational seating.

My, what singing we had. I was old enough to learn the songs and sing along with the rest of them. Sometimes, they would ask, "Does anyone in the congregation have a song picked for us to sing?" I would already have one. I would almost always pick "Where Could I Go but to the Lord." It got to be a habit for someone to ask me if I had a selection knowing which one I would choose.

The church was filled with people consoling others, stopping what they were doing every now and again for prayer. Everyone would be praying, even the children. They didn't believe in just say-ing a quick prayer; they believed in praying through, as I often heard my grandmother call that. There was never any time limit. It didn't matter if it was all day or all night. Some would pray until an answer came for whoever they were praying for. Those that felt the calling of the Spirit would lay hands on the person and pray. Even at my young age, I felt the importance of the Spirit touching me, and I would pray to myself. A lot of the children would be tired and sleepy, but we knew to have respect and kept quiet. Sometimes the small children would start whining or having temper tantrums from being tired and sleepy; some children would fall asleep. If they started to get a little rowdy, one of the older girls or the mothers who were not directly involved would take them to the outside or next door to the Aheart's house to get them to sleep. Mrs. Aheart had children of her own, so she understood and offered her living room and kitchen for this purpose. Also, during this time, the women could look in on the Aheart's teenage son; he was sick with cancer. He was bedfast. It would keep Mrs. Aheart from having to leave the service to look in on him.

The church congregation spent evenings on up into the night, praying for the boy to be healed. However, among all the people who did receive healing, he did not. It was a hard thing to hear him crying from being in pain. I could barely stand to think of him suffering like that.

Chapter 20

My grandfather, we called him Pa, Mother's father, passed away when I was three. Of all the memories during that age, I do not remember him. But my older sisters say that before they got the word of his death, and it would have been about the time of his death, they heard him walk across the porch and up to the door. When they went to the door, he was not there. It wasn't long after that happened that they got the word of his passing. Almost every person in our family had a gift; several people dreamed dreams, some had premonitions, and things like this were common. It was very ordinary for people to have a spiritual gift of some kind.

Mom, Dad, and all the small children were in bed fast asleep. Lona and Dona were up working on their embroidery. Lona was stitching a days-of-the-week pattern on her cotton dish towels. The pattern had a mother hen. The mother hen was busy doing a different chore each day of the week while her chicks played. Dona was busy stitching a floral design on pillowcases and dresser scarves. They looked at each other when they heard the footsteps of Pa coming up the steps and to the door. They both jumped up and tried to beat each other to the door. Lona was the fastest and flung the door open to great him. No one was there. At first, they thought he was playing a trick on them, but after they looked all over the place, and they could not find him. Pa had been sick for a while; he had stomach cancer. The next morning, Mom got the news. Pa had passed away at the exact time the girls heard the footsteps.

After Pa passed, Maw often lived with us. She was an incredibly special person in my life. She was often reading to us and teaching us songs. I never knew how she got that name. I guess someone could not say grandma, so they just said Maw, and that was good enough.

She carried around in her bags books to read to us, and when we were old enough to care for them and read them, she would give them to us. She had many books about Jesus and his life.

I had two favorite books I kept until I was nearly a grown-up and read them to my younger brothers and sisters. One was about a little girl who would not stay out of the chicken house and wanted to go look at the baby chicks. She wanted to hold them and pet them, upsetting the mother hen which upset the other hens as well. The little girl's mother told her time and time again to stay out of the chicken house. Then one day, she reached into the nest to get a baby chicken, but they were gone. She saw something move and looked in to find a big ugly black snake. Now go figure. How in the world did Maw find this book about this little girl who was so much like me? Who did she know that she could get to write this book about me?

Maxine age 4

Another book was about a little girl who would not leave her shoes on, beautiful black patent slippers. One day, she left them outside and forgot them. Later that evening, a rain came, and her black slippers got wet. When she was looking for her shoes the next morning, she remembered that she left them outside, and when she found them, they had shrunk, and her feet would not fit into them. Now this was not like me, and I wanted to make sure that I never did that. I was very careful to make sure it never happened to me.

Chapter 21

Dad thought that he had enough hay in store for the horses, mules, and cattle, but it had been a bad winter, and he was afraid that he would run short. Dad had been out doing the early morning chores when Mom rang the bell for him to know that she had breakfast on the table.

We were all seated at the table waiting for him as he entered the back porch. He hung his coat and hat on the hook and washed his hands and face in the basin of water that Mom had gotten ready for him; she always kept the bucket of water and a basin on a small table right near the back door of the porch. The porch was enclosed during the winter and screened during the summer.

He seated himself at the table and said grace, and as he began to help Mom with the smaller children, he said, "It has been a hard winter, and I have had to feed more than usual. I am afraid that I am going to run out of hay, and I really need to go get a load. I know that everyone else is facing the same thing. I will probably have a hard time finding some." He helped himself to another biscuit and started again, "I will have to check around to see where I can find someone who might have some they will sell. I know someone right across the creek who might have some. If not, I will have to go to Shoffner."

There were only two ways to get to Shoffner from where we lived if you did not want to go miles out of the way to get there. One was the footbridge; the other was through the creek.

"I will get the wagon ready and see if I can make it across the creek. If I can cross the creek, I will go on. By the time I come back, the water will have time to go down quite a bit, and I shouldn't have any trouble getting back through it even though I will have a load."

Mom agreed with him that he had to go. "I can't stand to think of those poor animals going hungry. We just can't take the risk."

When the water was up from rain, one could not get through either way. If you need something from the store, you had to go by way of the footbridge.

Dad looked at Gerald and said, "Okay, boy, you ready to go?"

Gerald jumped up, and his long legs got all tangled up, almost causing him to fall. "I'm ready, Dad, just give me a jiffy."

Nate whined, "I want to go."

Mom and Dad both spoke at the same time, "No, son."

Looking at the hurt in Nates eyes, Dad tried to explain. He got down on one knee and looked him in eyes and said, "Son, I am going to be gone most of the day, and you are the only man here to take care of Mom and these girls while I am gone. Do you think you can do that for me?"

Nate was satisfied with that.

Gerald told me a story about walking across the footbridge when the water was up so high that the bridge swayed until he could hardly stay on. He said that it was so scary to walk across that bridge. Dad would make him go to help him carry the groceries or supplies for the farm. He hated the footbridge when the water was up. Sometimes, it would be up to the bottom of the bridge. He was afraid to go across it at these times.

Dad had gotten across the creek with no trouble and found some hay in Shoffner. The water in the creek had gone down some but was still swelling. Gerald was riding on top of the hay. The wagon hit a large rock and jolted him off into the water. Dad was whistling and singing and didn't even know what had happened. No matter what task Dad was doing during the day, he would be whistling and singing as he worked. I loved just sitting and listening to him. Gerald yelled and yelled. The water was rolling so hard that he could not swim in it. He grabbed ahold of a limb, but it broke off. The water washed him further. He tried grabbing ahold of reeds; they broke also. He kept screaming for help as the water was washing him away. Under the water he went and back up to the top. Like a roller coaster, under and over, trying to yell for help and screaming, but the water would get unto his mouth until it was hard to do. How was he going to get out? How far would the water take him? This was the very thing that he had feared—the raging water that rolled angrily beneath the footbridge and what it would do if a foot slipped. And he slid off when the water had been so high under it that it made the footbridge sway back and forth.

Dad said something to Gerald about the water in the creek being higher and fiercer than he thought but didn't get a response. Dad said something else but still no response. He turned to see if Gerald maybe had fallen asleep, but he wasn't there. Dad turned the wagon around and started looking. After finally realizing that he had lost him off the hay wagon, he then heard Gerald's cries for help as he came near the creek. Faint cries against the sound of the raging water. He halted the team of horses and jumped off the wagon, running as fast as he could, and he leaped into the raging stream. Heaving himself forward in leaps and bounds, he was able to reach out for Gerald's hand and retrieved the boy from the swirling waters.

Drying the boy as best as he could and wrapping him in his coat, he put Gerald beside him on the buckboard and held onto him tightly as they journeyed on toward home. When Dad stopped the wagon, he hollered to Mom and told her to come quickly and bring a blanket. Mother ran to the nearest bedroom to grab a blanket and ran outside to see what was going on. All the older children ran with her, and everyone was asking at one at a time, "What happened? What on earth happened?" Gerald was blue and shivering. Dad grabbed him down from the buckboard, and Mom wrapped him in the blanket. Ma had seen what was going on from the house and had a warm towel ready. She had gotten a kitchen chair and put it near the stove and hung the towel over it to warm. The girls ran back into the house and automatically pitched in to help Ma as she gathered the clothes and warm towel. Dad carried him into the kitchen and sat him in a chair near the warm cookstove.

The boy welcomed warm dry clothes and a warm supper. He sat right up close to that warm stove to chase away the chills from that cold water while he devoured his supper and drank his warm cocoa.

"He's fine," Dad whispered. "Look how he is eating."

Mom gave a gentle chuckle, nodding her head.

All the children gathered around to listen as Dad tried to tell explain to Mom what happened.

Chapter 22

It was also while living here at this house that I remember learning to have respect for garden tools. We weren't allowed to play with those. We weren't old enough to use them without supervision. But we had been told how to care for them and the proper way to place them so no one would get hurt. We had even felt the results of not turning the hoe the right way when leaning it against the wall when we stepped on the blade, and it flipped backward and banged each of us in the head. We had laughed at each other when we got that lesson. We were incredibly careful about leaving it lying on the ground. Nathaniel and I had each been taught that lesson as well when we tripped and fell over it. We didn't dare leave it lying with the sharp part of the blade turned up for one of us or someone else to step on. We knew how sharp it was; we had seen our dad sharpen the blade and then test it on some weeds.

We were getting ready for a visit with some of our cousins. Dad and the younger children cleaned the yard and porch. Mom, Lona, and Dona cooked up a lot of food. This was a large family also. Most of the time, they came on the weekends and spent the night. There were several boys as well as girls. The boys seemed too rowdy for me. I do remember playing hide-and-seek and other games outside. Then someone had been playing with the garden hoe and left it turned upside down. The boys were really geared up and chasing each other round and round the house. Then one of them started screaming very loudly, wailing like nothing I have heard before. When the adults went to inspect the situation, they found Billy with his toes sliced almost all the way off the foot where he had stepped on the hoe. Well, I don't know why or whoever got it out and had taken a notion to get into the garden shed and drag it out. It seemed that they were having enough fun and were certainly busy enough, but I thought that that was a dumb thing to do.

The women went back to sharing recipes, and Mom got to show off her canned foods stacked on the shelf Dad had built for her that she loved to display on. As she would take her jar out of the canners, she would wipe each jar off and hold it up and smile. She would often say, "Now isn't that pretty?" She took a lot of pride in all that work. She would always have extra, so she could say, "Here, take this jar and try it." She often would have a jar of jelly, pickles, some sort of relish, or soup. She loved also to show off some little dress that she had saved a flour sack or sugar sack to make. The women saved the cotton sacks until they had enough of the same color or pattern to make a shirt or dress for a child. They often traded the patterns or colors to help each other get enough of a certain one that they had been wanting.

The men continued their conversations on the front porch about the war that had not been over but a few years. They talked about the harm it had done on our economy and how jobs were getting harder to find. Jobs that paid a salary well enough so that you could provide for your family. They smoked some tobacco that Grandpa had tried his hand at growing. It wasn't all that bad, but it took too much caring for than they had time to fool with. Daddy made a pot of coffee with some chicory that he had picked up. He thought he would mix it with his coffee to make it last longer. During the war, it was all they could get, and most people could barely afford it. Some had to grind acorns to use for coffee. Some of the men really liked the chicory and some did not. Although it wasn't that bad, they still preferred regular coffee.

By this time, the women were settled at the table waiting on the coffeepot to perk their fresh pot of coffee without the chicory. I watched the brown water perk up from the tube in the middle of the basket. This always fascinated me. When the coffee had perked enough to suit Momma, she poured it into the cups. The women put it into their saucers and drank it from the saucer because it was so hot. Some of the children wanted to drink that brown rich-looking liquid. Mom took out a small tea set from the cupboard. A friend of

Maw's had given it to her for Joyce and I. Occasionally, we would have a tea party. Momma took the little teapot and poured some water into it and then a little of the coffee. She put in some cream and sugar. We watched as she added some vanilla and poured that caramel-colored liquid into our cups. Then she went to the cook-stove and retrieved some biscuits from the stove warmer. She had made extra biscuits for snacks for when the children got hungry later. She always made extra biscuits.

She told the children, "Now dip your biscuit into your coffee and taste it."

"Oh, my!" said one of the children. "I have never tasted anything so good."

Summer had gone and the cotton fields were ready to be picked. There was a field of cotton right across the road from our house. Mr. Churchill had asked if we wanted to pick the cotton. It was not a large field, and all his laborers had other fields to pick, and he was running out of helpers for this field too. Momma said that Daddy had his obligations to the farmer that he worked for, but she and Essom and his family would be happy to help. They came to stay with us until the field was picked. It was him and Maw, his wife Icie, Aunt Amy, and Momma. They had their little boy, Melvin, and Momma had me and Joyce all to the fields with them. Nathaniel, Gerald, Lona, and Dona went to school.

When we got tired, Momma, Maw, or one of the others would take us little ones to sit under a huge black walnut tree and rest. Sometimes, we would get to lay on their cotton sacks, and they pulled us along. Melvin and Joyce would fall asleep. Mr. Churchill came by on the way to the cotton gin with a load of cotton picked from another field. He gave Essom a large canvas tarp and told him to spread it on the ground to empty their sacks of cotton onto when they got full. He would get a wagon to them as soon as he could. But the cotton would be okay on the tarp until he got back with a wagon. That way, they would not have to wait on him to empty their cotton sacks. They had a huge pile of cotton before he got the wagon to them.

Mr. Churchill told Momma that she could have all those black walnuts that she wanted. He had tasted Momma's baking at some of the church socials and knew that she favored the flavor of the black walnut in some of her cakes. Later after cotton picking was over, Nathaniel and I picked up black walnuts in a toe sack, and everyone helped to take the nut out of the shells for Momma to use in her baking. They were also good for medicine, especially the dried hulls. They made a juice that was good for skin ailments. Dad took nails and flattened them at the sharp end with the hammer. This made a handy tool to dig the nut out of the shell. As we cracked the shell of the walnuts, the nut was hard to get out on most of them. We loved to eat these nuts and did until we had our fill.

Chapter 23

don't remember the move, as in the actual moving day. I do remember the whining and sighing when we were told that we were moving, but the next memories that I have was at the age of five.

House that I was born

We had moved back into the house that we had lived in at the time of my birth. I had a new brother born in February 9, 1952. Loyd Dale is his name. I don't even remember the event. I just remember how special he was, and we were both born in the same house.

I cried because Gerald and Nathaniel got to go to school, and I did not. They walked down the long road out to the main highway to catch the school bus. My, how I wanted to ride that big yellow school bus. Mom let me walk down the road with them to catch the bus, but when I started trying to get on the bus, she made me quit going. Oh, I was mad at them because they had complained about me trying to get on the bus with them.

I had often complained, "I don't know why we have had to move so much." But I knew that my father was a farm laborer, and he worked for whoever needed him. Or maybe whoever could pay the most money and had the best benefits. A lot of the small farmers were selling out and finding work with some of the factories in Newport. Some of them were moving up north to go to work in the automobile factories. Times were getting harder for the small farmer and the farm laborer to make a living.

I remember Dad often mentioning the benefits. When he would talk to someone about a job, he would discuss the work, money, and benefits with Mom, like a house and electricity, barnyard, corn, and hay for the animals. I had heard Mom and Dad talking about work, and Dad had said that there wasn't much work to be found. He would have to take whatever he could find. Sometimes, the houses were not that good, and they were too small for our family, but we made do with whatever was provided for us.

Chapter 24

I loved this homeplace. I loved the barnyard and the animals, the chicken yard and the chickens, white rabbits. And the fields. This was the house that I was born in.

I asked Dad what the steps were doing by the gate that went over the fence. He told me that when we lived here before, the gate was too hard for Lona and Dona to open, and often they did not get it closed well, and the animals would get out. So he built the steps over it, so they could get across to help him and Momma with the barnyard chores.

The White River ran not far off and, as the last place we lived in, I loved to go there with the family.

That was the first time I had seen an electric eel and feared the water after I heard the stories of how it had shocked people to death. This was the not first I had heard of an electric current and was a little unsure of how it could be in a fish or the water. But their stories were so convincing that I took their word for it and never questioned it again.

I was amazed at all the forest creatures and their nature. This was my first up close encounter with a baby squirrel and raccoon. I learned soon that they had a quick and sharp bite.

Dad, being the hunter that he was and often working in the log woods, would sometimes come home with a young forest creature or two. Once he brought a baby raccoon that had somehow lost its mother. It was quite the pet, very comical and playful. As it grew older, it became a dominant little creature and thought it was the boss. He often tried to attack, and when he got ahold of someone, he would claw badly and sometimes bite. Dad was afraid he would get ahold of one of the children, so he took him back to the woods and let him go.

Daddy brought home the baby squirrel that he found in a nest in a tree. We kept them in a cage. Sometimes, we took them out to play with them. But they, like the raccoon, had that dominant nature. They were not as bad, but if they decided to bite, those small but sharp teeth would go all the way through your finger. Dad had made a cage and put a wheel in it, so they could play on it. We loved to sit and watch them play, but they got too mean, so back to the woods with them too.

Daddy also brought home hedge apples. They were large green balls. He let us play with some of them. If we hit them with a ball bat, they busted open and smelled bad. Hedge apple trees made a natural fence because they were big and strong and had thorns growing on them. The oils in the hedge apples were used to keep pests, such as spiders and mice, away from the house, sheds, and barns. Momma would not let Dad bring them in the house because the oil had a smell. Some people don't mind the smell and used them for ornaments. They may have used them for ornaments to repel the flies.

We thought that Daddy knew a lot of strange things. He also would find a beechnut tree and chew the bark. We thought he was chewing gum. When we begged him for it, he couldn't give it to us because Momma would not let him; she was afraid it would make us sick. "Maybe when Dad goes to the store, he can bring you home some gum," Mom said the next day he came home with some regular beechnut gum. He chewed the bark to clean his teeth. We thought that he learned some of these things from his mother and her parents who were from the Cherokee Indian tribe.

Chapter 25

This was the year of my first real encounter with the garden work that came with it. As a helper during canning time. Not as that little child begging to get to help then growing tired and being able to run off to play, but a real helper.

I never forgot the process of canning beets and new potatoes. It was scrubbing the skin off those new potatoes that I hated. I was afraid that the skin would fall off my fingers. After helping with washtubs of carrots, potatoes, and beets; it was time for washing, scrubbing, cutting the tops off, and trimming the roots. There were washtubs full of water to carry, and the older kids would carry washtubs or a foot tub full of vegetables for us to work up, then Mom or Maw would come and take them to the kitchen to can. Gerald, Dona, and Lona would often come and help Nathaniel and I. Dad would often come and check our work and pitch in to help.

Dad and Gerald dug the potatoes, and the girls shook off the dirt and filled a bucket. They would fill the bucket and pour it into a tub. When it was full, they brought it to us to be scrubbed. They had the same routine with the beets and carrots. We thought the scrubbing would never end. When we were not doing that, we had to wash jars. Maw and Mom kept the water on the stove boiling. Water for washing and rinsing the jars had to be hot. Mom said, the water had to be hot so it would kill bacteria. If a jar had any kind of bacteria on it, then the vegetables in the jar would spoil. Even a speck of dirt or rust was not acceptable. We could hardly keep our hands in the water it was so hot, so Nathaniel and I didn't have to do much of that.

The green beans weren't a picnic either or shelling peas. I did not like looking over each side of the leaves of the different kinds of greens for bugs; there must be a better way to do all this, but everyone in the family—male or female—had to help when it was canning time. Mom and Dad made two gardens. They would save the greens and some of the other vegetables for the last garden. Some of the vegetables like the beans and potatoes, the ones we ate a lot of, they planted in both gardens. Early garden and late garden.

Then again, it was time to butcher hogs, chickens, or rabbits. We did not get to visit the smokehouse very often, but when we did, it was sheer pleasure just to breath in the aroma.

Every so often, chickens were dressed out for market. Mom or my sisters would dress them out, and Dad delivered them to the customers. Sometimes, Dad would let me ride with him. I would wait happily in the car while he delivered the chickens to each customer. There was one of the lady costumers who had a fit on Daddy because Mom cut the tail of her chicken. That was just what Mom did when she cleaned them. But I specificity remembered Mom telling Dad, "This hen goes to Mrs. Baker. Make sure that she gets this one. She doesn't want the tail cut off her hen." Mom had repeated, "She likes the tail left on her hen. Now don't get them mixed up." That is just what he did, and he had two ladies upset at him. I couldn't help but laugh at him when he got back to the car.

"I want you to know that I got those hens mixed up after your mom warning me...," he said.

Both women griped at Mom for his mistake and said that if he couldn't beat that, they were going to stop buying their hens from them. Needless to say, Mom was upset at him at first but then laughed about it, and to make him feel better, she told him, "Don't worry, Lee, if those two old hens don't want any more hens after you apologized to them and you took the trouble to go back and switched hens with them, then I will just sell my hens to someone else." And they laughed because she called them old hens.

Mom did not buy all her groceries from the store in town. She often bought supplies from Mr. Sexton, who ran the rolling store. He would stop in front of people's house, and they would go into his store and shop. It was a long van setup with groceries on shelves for display, just like in a store. People would go in and pick out whatever they needed. He also had a list of things that they could order, and he would bring them the next time he came around. He came this route once a week. He carried a great supply of Watkins flavorings, spices, and pie fillings. Mom always bought these things from him when she needed them. He had almost anything in that rolling store as he did in his store in Bradford, the town he was from. Sometimes, Mr. Sexton would buy eggs and chicken from Mom. Then sometimes they would trade, occasionally he would ask her to bake him a cake or a pie.

One day, Mr. Sexton's truck hit Mom's big red rooster. He brought it up to the house, and as he handed it to her, he said, "Ador"—that is what everyone called her—"I accidently hit your rooster. I tried to miss him but couldn't. I sure am sorry. He sure would make some good dumplings if you want to dress him out and cook him."

She looked sort of sad but replied to him, "Oh, I know that he was going to get hit by someone the way he liked to get in that road. Yes, you are right, he would make some good dumplings. I got company coming tomorrow. That is just what I will cook."

There was also a small country store down the road from where we lived. Maudelene Turner's store. Mom and Dad did a lot of their shopping there in between the times they could buy from the rolling store or go to town. When they did make the trip to town, they tried to stock up well on supplies, so they wouldn't have to buy much in between, unless it was something they needed that they could only find at the rolling store or Madelene's store.

We loved to go into the rolling store. We would listen for him to come rolling down the road, and he would ring his loud bell, so people could know he was near. Most of the time, Momma went to meet him; sometimes she would send Nathaniel and me with a list. Mr. Sexton would give us a sucker or some bubble gum. We would pop the gum into our mouths and look at the comic paper it had been wrapped in all the way home. Neither of us could read yet. When we got home, someone would read it to us. If Gerald was around, he would and then beg us for the wrappers. He collected them and kept them in a wooden box that someone had given him. Sometimes, when putting the wrappers in, he would proudly show us his display. He would lay them out in the order with the correct character and read us the story. He explained about comic books, and how when you had the right wrappers that when put together, they told a story.

Nathaniel and I were always ready for a story; we loved to have someone read to us or listening to people tell stories. Our parents and grandparents were always talking about some of the ancestors and how things used to be. When we asked questions about it, we would always get a story. Maw had a story about one of our Indian ancestors from Grandpa Swearingen's line. I thought it was a beautiful story but a sad one too. Her name was Pocahontas, an Indian princess.

Pocahontas was born in Wicomico, Virginia. She was named Meto-aka and later Pocahontas, which means playful little girl. Meto-aka was only used when she was in the tribe. The first time she met White men, she met Capt. John Smith. He was injured in a battle with another Indian tribe. Pocahontas found him and took him to her tribe where he made friends and stayed until he was healed. She often saw Captain John Smith when she visited Jamestown to take furs for her father, Chief Powhatan, and other goods that the tribe had to trade. Their friendship grew stronger. There was another English captain in the settlement that watched Pocahontas and planned to kidnap her. He captured her and held her for ransom. She was eventually taken to and held in a settlement where she met a young tobacco farmer, Sir Thomas Rolfe. She began to be an advocate between the people in the settlement and her tribe. During her captivity, she was encouraged to convert to Christianity and was baptized under the name Rebecca. Her father bargained with the colonist for her release. She married the tobacco planter John Rolfe in April 1614 at the age of about seventeen, and she had a son, Thomas Rolfe, when she was eighteen. Her husband had to go on a voyage to London, England, seeking James and Queen Anne. There she was, surprised to see her friend Captain John Smith talking to them. He introduced her to the king and queen. They were in England for seven months before returning home. Pocahontas grew sick from all the dampness in London and could not make the voyage home. She died on the ship. As she lie dying, she tried to comfort her husband by saying, "All must die. Is it not enough that the child lived?" They turned to shore, and she was buried in a church yard of the St. Mary, the virgin church in Norfolk, England.

*****

I stood watching as Dad showed Nathaniel how to skin a squirrel and a rabbit, and Dad explained to him the difference and why it made a difference. Everything seemed to have a different way of being dressed or canned or stored. Just as they had a different way of being cared for. Even different kinds of fish were dressed out differently.

I wanted to do it next.

"No, you are too little. Besides, you are a girl."

I cried and begged until he gave in. He hung the animals for me and looked on to supervise. Much to his amazement, I did remember what I had seen, even though I needed a little help from him to get the job done.

"I guess you can," he said. He pretty much let me do as I pleased and was so gentle and patient about it.

I loved the sugarcane fields. There is nothing like the taste of a sample of sugarcane right out of the field.

Dad had warned us, "Don't go near the sugarcane, and remember how the blades from the corn stalks cut?"

Nathaniel replied, "Oh, yes, we sure do."

I repeated him like an echo, and I really did not, but I believed that Nathaniel really did remember the sting from the cuts on his flesh. He said, "Remember, Dad hadn't wanted us to follow him." But we kept on until he agreed to let us follow him just a little way into the cornfield as he checked the corn. It was enough to teach us a lesson. The leaves from the stalks cut your skin too. It was rough trying to follow him. I did not like it at all.

Now he said, "If you remember that, then remember this: the stalks on the sugarcane are even sharper, and they will slice like a knife." We never even had a desire to test that; we knew about knives. Our brother Gerald had sliced his leg to the bone trying to sharpen his pocketknife. We were all sitting around the woodstove one night, talking, laughing, and Dad whistling. Gerald was sharpening his knife with a white stone that our uncle had given him. At the time, he was around the age of eight or nine. Then there was a sudden "Ouch!" and we all turned to look at Gerald. He was gripping his knee, and his pants was turning crimson.

Dad said, "Boy, what have you done?"

Mother was not one to panic, but she said, "Oh, lord." That was always her expression at something more severe.

Maw said, "Dear Jesus." Neither was she one to panic.

Then Dad said, "Well, let's have a look." By this time, he already had Gerald's hand pried off and pants torn open at the slit. He did not wait for him to take them off; he just ripped them open.

I guess he could tell it was bad by the way the crimson stain was crawling down his leg. Next thing he said was "To the bone."

Mother said, "Oh, Lord," and Maw said, "Dear Jesus." They both had already gathered the necessary bandages and coal oil, which was the medication for that type of thing in those days. Needle, thread, and boiling water, then a coal of fire to sterilize the needle. I think they were able to wrap it tight enough that they didn't have to sew. When Gerald thought they were going to have to, he cried like a baby.

Dad said, "Suck it up, boy. You will be more careful the next time." Then Dad said to Mom, "Where did he get this?"

Mom said, "I thought you gave it to him."

They turned to Gerald, and he replied, "Uncle Essom gave it to me."

Maw said, "I will get on to him for giving something like that to that boy."

Dad replied to her, "Now, now, there is nothing wrong with him giving those things to him. He is plenty old enough for it. He just didn't know how to use them." He showed Gerald the correct way to sharpen his knife. That was the last time he ever had to say anything about knives to any of us. They were well respected from that day on.

Chapter 26

I don't know which I liked better, the taste of the sugarcane right out of the field or the honey dripping right from the cone. Dad would go hunting and sometimes come back with honey from a beehive inside an old tree with.

I remember him talking about getting the honey, asking him questions, listening to his answers. He would watch the hive for days until just the right time to take the honey. When Mom would get all the honey from the cone, Dad would remind her to save some of the cone for us to chew on. You couldn't swallow it, just chew it until the sweet is gone. Oh my! What a treat.

The amazing thing was how everything had to be done in its own way, and there was a specific reason for that. Just as all the vegetables and fruits had an order for getting them ready for canning or drying to be stored in the cellar or whatever the case be.

As young as I was, it did not bother me to see the animals butchered. It was a necessity for our survival. It was the way things were, and the people in those days did not vary from that fact. You grew livestock for food and market just like you did a vegetable in the garden or the crops in the field.

I remember how each was dressed out from that age, as most youngsters back then did.

You learned from watching and helping, if they let you or made you just as soon as they thought you could do even a little to help.

It seemed though that work was not all that bad. We sang songs, told jokes, and teased. Some of the older people often told stories. Sometimes, we had tournaments to see who could do most in a certain length of time. There was only one prize, and that was the satisfaction of knowing that you had won.

Gerald and Nathaniel walked down the long lane to catch that big yellow school bus. I wanted to go with them. Sometimes, Momma would let me, but she had to stop after I tried to go to school with them, then I thought I would just wait there until they got home. Well, that didn't work with Mom when she had to come down the road to get me. She didn't get mad at me, she just stopped letting me go, and that broke my heart.

Chapter 27

O ne of my favorite stories is about my oldest sister. My parents spoke often about the story of Lona and the lima bean. This incident happened when Lona was around two and a half years of age, and Dona was around one year.

As the story goes, it was late in the day. Supper had been served and the kitchen cleaned. Mother and Dad both had another task to attend to. She was setting at the table, shelling lima beans for canning the next day. Dad was bringing in fresh water, wood for the heat stove, and seeing that the animals were put to bed for the night. The girls were playing but becoming ready for bath and bed.

Lona had become more fretful than usual. Mom was wondering if she might be coming down with a cold; after all, she kept rubbing her nose.

When Mom had finished with the lima beans, she put them in water to soak overnight for the next day cooking. Dad finished with his chores just in time to help finish up Mom's task while she attended to the girls. Lona whimpered as Mom dressed her for bed.

Mom said to Dad, "I am afraid Lona is coming down with an ailment. She is awful fretful."

Dad took her and sang "Rock-a-Bye Baby" as he rocked her. Mom put Dona to bed, and she fell asleep right away. She did not stay asleep for long. Lona's whimpers turned into cries, and the crying soon turned into wailing.

Lona's nose was runny, so Mom and Dad were sure that she had caught a cold. But she kept sticking her little finger up in her nose and digging around, so Dad thought he would look to see what might be wrong, and there he saw it. A lima bean. It had swollen up from the moisture created from the crying, which made the runny nose. He tried to get her to blow her nose. That did not get it out. With all the crying, it made her nose run. Even more, the bean had swollen up. The two parents grew weary with the crying of the two babies. They did not know what to do. Whatever they tried, they could not get Lona to cooperate.

There was only one thing to do. So they bundled the two children up and started on foot to Maw and Paw's house. That would be Mother's parents' house. Unfortunately, our grandparents lived on the very top of the mountain, and we lived at the bottom. I believe it has been told that it was the highest mountain around Mountain View, Arkansas.

Well, off they went, in the middle of the night, on foot with two crying babies. They were more than halfway up the mountain when suddenly, Lona stopped crying and held out her hand. "See," she said in a calm little voice. The bean had fallen out. They all laughed and decided there was only one thing to do, keep going. Surely by this time, Maw and Paw would already be up and have the coffee brewing. Maybe, just maybe, they would be so glad to see their sweet little granddaughters that they would care for them while Mom and Dad got a little rest before their walk back down the mountain.

What a great Sunday service. There were a lot of people at church today. We had special quest singers. We often had a few quests from Cleburne County and Stone County. Several people in our church were from that area, the mountains, and like Mom and Dad. Many of these families, were also our relation. They had moved down to the bottoms to be closer to work. Most of our family played some kind of musical instrument and sang. This occasion was that we had a very special quest that was a good friend of our family. His name was Wayne Rainey. I loved when he came. After service, he always came to the house. Mom would always have food cooked, and everyone would play their instruments and sing. There was nothing like that mountain music. He gave me a harmonica and showed me how to play it. I felt special to have received such a treat from such a well-known musician as Mr. Wayne Rainey.

We had a great gathering at the house, mostly with church family which included many of our relatives also.

All the children were playing hide-and-seek when we were all pulled onto the porch for a little talk by some of our parents. "Now, children, we don't care where you hide as long as it is safe and nothing gets torn up. The only thing that we want you to beware of is if you happen to see any kind of powder or anything at all that you don't know is safe, do not touch it. Listen to us now. The little Harris girl, you all know her, well, she was hiding in the stove warmer"—the pastor pointed to Mom's stove warmer that she had traded out, and it was sitting on the porch and some of the smaller children like myself had hid inside it. "Well, she dropped her gum in some powder inside a lid that was hid in there. She picked it back up and stuck it in her mouth."

"Uh-huh," someone said.

"Now listen, children," he said, "I know that some of you know not to, but everyone may not. We just want to make sure that everyone knows better, so they won't do it. That was rat poison she dropped her gum into, and it took her life. Do you all understand the danger? The best thing is if you drop your gum or piece of candy, do not pick it up because it is dirty. But you don' know what it may have landed in. Don't be putting anything in your mouth. Okay?"

Some of us did know he dangers and did wonder why we had not seen that little girl around, but we did not know what had happened to her, and we were incredibly sad for her family and for her.

Chapter 28

oving time again… I did not want to leave this house that I loved so well, though we just moved across the road.

"Why do we have to move, Mom?"

She replied, "We must go where the work is."

The house was surrounded by a bean field on three sides. The house was almost surrounded by a cotton field. The backyard was taken up by a spot for the garden, pigpen, chicken yard, and chicken house, and a place for the rabbit cages. Essentials for living.

The south side was so small and close to the bean field that we weren't allowed to play there. That side also was where Momma grew her flowers, mostly roses. Oh, how we did love Momma's roses. We loved all her flowers just like she did. They were a part of her.

She loved each thing—her garden of vegetables, chickens, rabbits—and babied everything just as if they were one of her babies. She smiled at them and talked to them so tenderly just like she did her children. Now she never liked those fifthly pigs. But accepted them because she knew they were essential to the welfare of her family.

My parents, Maw, our older brother, and sisters picked cotton across the road from the house. We were left at the house. Every few minutes, someone would come to the house to check on us smaller children. Dad and the others picked the rows in the field, and Mom and Maw picked the ends of their rows closer to the house, so she could watch us. By the time her row began to reach out a little further, she would turn back on another row, leaving the rest for the others.

Dad had a contract with the owner of the cotton crop. He had to get the cotton picked by a certain time. So he needed as much help as he could get.

Chapter 29

Nathaniel was seven by this time. I was five. Joyce was two, and Loyd was a toddler. Sometimes, Mom would put him on the end of her pick sack and let him ride or let him play along the row as she picked.

It never failed; we would be doing something that made a big mess. We would get a scolding, and the next time she checked, it would be something different. Another scolding.

Momma was very particular about her house and always got up early to have everything in order before she went to the field. She loved to sew and do fine needlework. She took great pride to see that it was perfect. She made all her curtains, bedspreads, quilts, tablecloths, scarves for tables, and dressers. Also pillows and coverings for her couches and chairs and such as that. She kept them clean, starched, and ironed. How on earth she did that with all us children, I have never been able to master.

She came in once and found us jumping on the bed. We had her bed unmade. There were pillows and bed coverings in the floor where we had jumped off the bed to land upon on. We had pulled the curtains off the window because we had to hang onto them to keep from falling when we climbed on top of the headboard to jump off. Just jumping off the bed had become boring. We needed a better challenge, and we had even been climbing off the top of the wardrobe cabinet.

My, did we get in trouble. We had been promised fifty cents for being good. And we had planned just how we were going to spend it. We lost it. That was worse than the spanking Nathaniel and I got. Joyce didn't get a spanking. Momma said that we were supposed to be setting the example for her.

To make matters worse, she just quit and stayed home for the day, and when Dad came home for lunch, she told him, and we got in trouble again. She left the mess. We thought she left it for him to see. Anyway, that was what she told us. Later, I realized that the truth was she didn't have time to straighten it up because she had to prepare lunch for a family of nine people.

We all straightened up the house together. Everyone helped. From that time on, Mom had some of the older children stay closer to the house with her, so they could check even more often to see what we were doing. They also let us go to the field with them at times. They were good at making a game out of work, and like all children, we wanted to help. Mom gave Nathaniel a pillow sack. That was his pick sack. He was thrilled to no end. I pouted because I was not allowed to have a sack as well. Mom let me pick handfuls and put it in her sack. Joyce and Loyd played.

Chapter 30

We were told if we were good and did an excellent job helping, we could have back the money we had lost due to bad behavior.

But we knew exactly what we would spend our money on. We had planned it all out before we lost it.

I still remember the day when Dad got his pay. Everyone in the house was ready to climb onto the buckboard when he came in the house and said, "Let's go to town. Everybody ready?"

I loved those days when we got to go to town. Newport was an exciting city to me. I loved it. Although I only went to two stores, the hardware and merchandise store and the drugstore. The mercantile store had everything that a person would want or need. Groceries, hardware, clothing, garden and yard tools, seeds, and toys. Yeah! Toys.

Across the street at the drugstore, it was ice cream and sodas. Sometimes, we would have burger and chips; sometimes it was just for a glass of ice water. Oh my! The ice water was so clear and cold. So delicious. At times, I preferred that over the Coca-Cola and Cherry Coke. Or lemonade.

Gerald talked about the hot tamales that he bought from a vender on the street. They were so good. He also went to the movies, him and Nathaniel.

Mom bought the hot tamales too to take home for us every time we went to town. They were so good. We looked forward to them. Then someone spread around a rumor that the old man who made the hot tamales had made them out of stray cats. The younger children cried because Mom wouldn't buy them anymore. We didn't care what they were made of; they were good.

"Where are we going?" we were asking as they were getting us dressed in our church clothes.

"We are going to a funeral," Dad said.

"Whose funeral?" we asked.

"Well, do you remember that little girl that lived up the road there on the curve by the water?"

Yes, we did.

"Well," he said. "The other day, as the family was going to town, she was sitting by the door looking out the window and accidently got the door open and fell out of the car. Her head hit a rock, and it killed her."

Oh, how sad, we thought.

I had heard Dad tell Mom that it busted her little head open, and her brains spilled out on the road. I thought that was the most horrible thing. I felt so sad.

At the funeral, she lay in the casket so still, dressed in the most beautiful long white dress, and she had a headband made of elite and yellow flowers with ribbons hanging down on the sides of her head. Momma cried as she walked by the casket, leading me by the hand. She was one of the distant relatives that lived in the community. I wanted to cry too.

We followed the long line of vehicles to the cemetery. This was the same cemetery that some of our relatives had been buried. After the service, Mom and Maw went to the graves of Grandpa Swearingen, Grandma Matti, and Grandpa Thomas Vance.

This little girl had lived where my friend, James Easter, lived. He was Nathaniel's age, but he loved me like I was his own sister. I never knew what happened to him until I was a grown-up, and they told me that he had passed away from some terrible illness. I had lost a few friends when I was very young. And even as young as five, I realized that death had no respect of age. We had had the teenager that drowned in the creek. I did not know that boy, but I knew what happened to him and how young he was. Then the Aheart boy who had cancer, the little girl who dropped her gum in rat poison, and now this little girl who fell out the door of the car. We were not afraid of death though.

Chapter 31

A short time after all the cotton was picked, my dad had purchased a truck. He had taken a job at Newport. Every day you could hear his truck long before it turned off the main highway off on the road to our house. I waited in the yard and listened and then ran to tell my mom that Dad was close to home. Ring started barking even before I could hear Dad's truck. I knew when he started barking that I could soon hear that truck.

Dad had been laid off at the plant he worked at and was working for a farmer. Well, the farmer that Dad worked for had told him that the crops had not been good, and he was afraid he wasn't going to run the risk next fall. Dad had taken a job at a plant in town, but they had a layoff. Many of the people we knew had already gone, people that were sharecroppers as my dad was or just had their own small acreage and could not make a living on it.

Dad went to town to make sure the truck was serviced and new tires were purchased. He wanted everything packed for loading as soon as he returned. The only sad thing is that we had to leave old Ring behind just like the neighbors before. But Dad had spoken to a neighbor who was willing to take the poor dog in. Ring was an old dog inherited from some neighbors who had gone up north to work in the canning factories. His name was Ring. He was all black except for a white ring around his neck. He followed me all the time and watched after me. If he thought I was going near danger or even if I was doing something I shouldn't, he would bark until Mom would come to look. I loved him even though he did get me in trouble at times.

The truck was loaded, and we were off like many other families, traveling to the north for the job that awaited there. Dad had contacted someone who said they had work. There was no work here at home, so we had to go.

The truck had sideboards built high up on the sides and over the tailgate. It was packed in a way that it would hold some of the older children, and they had a place to sit on. At nighttime, the truck was pulled over on the side of the road and some mattresses were taken off the truck and put on the grass beside the truck, and we rested until morning. Before we had left the house, Momma and Maw had prepared food to eat on the trip.

Chapter 32

When we arrived at the jobsite somewhere in Michigan, a house had been prepared for us. It was tiny. Just enough room for the bare necessities. Just enough room to eat and sleep.

After we were unloaded and settled in, Dad went to see the landlord about the work schedule for the next day. Soon, he was back at the small house. Mother had supper prepared. When we sat down to eat, he broke the news: We were going to have to look for work elsewhere. We were there for the strawberry crops. There had been a misfortune for the crop owners, and they had not grown as well as usual. Perhaps due to a bad winter. There would be little work. Our family could not live on what little Dad could make from the work provided for the labors. I looked around the table at the heads hanging low. I didn't have to see the look in their eyes; I could tell by the way they hung their heads that it was very sad and disappointing news.

We were not the only family who had met the misfortune. The grown-ups were all talking among each other, discussing what they were going to do, while the younger people talked and played games.

This was not the first time that we lived in Michigan. I don't remember much about the first time, but I remember visiting someone who lived in a house that had a huge red barn on a hillside. There were orchards there on that farm, and the people sent fruits home with us. I remember a huge diner with lots of people who all had children, and most of the people were from back home just like us. And just like home, the children played and laughed on into the night while the grown-ups visited. Then one by one, the different families would head on back to their own houses. What a good time everyone seemed to have, talking and laughing all the way home.

We had to go onto yet another job. Dad had found a job in Indiana, and I had no idea where this was. It seemed like a long way, and it was.

Chapter 33

When we arrived at the place prepared for us, it was a huge long building with room after room. People were already living there. We had four large rooms. A large room was prepared for a living room and a kitchen together. The rest of the rooms were bedrooms. One for my parents, one for my Maw, the other room was for all six of the children. Lloyd, since he was a baby, stayed with Mom and Dad.

We did not like this, but that was the way it was, so we adjusted. Soon settled in, we began to meet the neighbors. Unlike the other places where almost all the neighbors were people we already knew from home, these people were from different states. I had never heard of these places before, Virginia, Ohio, Missouri.

One family that we grew to know best was from Virginia. They talked about being from a tobacco farm. I did not even know what a tobacco was. They had two children, a boy and a girl. Someone for us to play with.

We lived right across form a canning factory. This was where the grown-ups worked. There were big trucks coming in and going out all day long, delivering truckloads of vegetables for canning.

On the weekend, the factory was closed, and all the people were at home. Many of the big trucks stopped coming in and going out. However, some still came, especially trucks transporting corn and tomatoes. Sometimes, truckloads of corn came during the night, and the tomatoes usually came in during early morning hours of Sunday.

The children played on the big loading dock. Chasing each other and playing hide-and-seek among the boxes and skids. Sometimes, there were large, empty iron wagons that we played on. We had lots of fun. We had no playground; the children were left to amuse themselves however they could.

Sometimes on the weekends, we would get to go to the park and play. That is one of my most favorite memories of our Maw. She often took us to the park to play and never without a picnic. Some of the grown-ups would take turns watching us while the others attended to the shopping for our staples.

Another one of our favorite places to go was with Dad to get the truck serviced. They let us stay in the truck when it went up on the rack. Now that was a joyride for us smaller children.

The older children went to see a movie while all this was going on. Almost like it was on a Saturday at home.

Chapter 35

A telephone call came for Dad. The people that lived in the camp that we lived in didn't have a phone, but there was a pay phone at the factory. The phone rang, and I was near, so I answered it. Someone was asking for Dad. I ran to get him. He returned and told us that he couldn't understand what the person was saying, but he thought that something was wrong with his mother. This was his stepmother, of course, but he had come to love her like his own mother. He decided to take a trip back to Arkansas to see what was going on. He was gone longer than Mom expected him to be. She was worried but also mad. Before he got back, all the work where we were at had ended, and Mom was wondering how we were going to get home.

Finally, Dad arrived and all I remembered was a story how he did not have the money to go back and had to sell the truck to buy a bus ticket. Then he got on the wrong bus and had gotten lost. The phone call was only someone he knew asking about the work, but he did not understand what they were saying, so he had to go back home and check it out. Mom was angry with him for days. All the other people living in that long row of rooms that we lived in had already left for their homes. We sold what we could and packed up the rest and headed for the bus stop to catch a bus back home. What a journey. Every time we had to change buses, I was afraid we would get on the wrong bus and get lost.

I do not remember arriving at our destination or what happened after we got there until just a few days before I started school.

We moved into a house in a little community called Bay, Arkansas. My dad worked for a farmer. That was where I lived when I started school, my first year. I was so excited to get to finally go to school. Even though my first year was not the best, I learned right away that I could not trust all people. Most of them were just not what I was used to being around. First, I was late getting started to school. All the other children had already chosen their friends, so that left me alone. Occasionally, a girl would play for a while but would be afraid to make her friends mad at her, so she would return to her group.

One day, the teacher called us up to the front of the classroom to sing a song. We held hands and went around in circles as we sang. We would stop and go again. When we stopped this time, there was a puddle of water between the boy that was holding my hand and myself.

I nudged him and said, "Look in the floor."

He began to try to alert the teacher, but she did not want him to be interrupted until some of the children started pointing and saying, "Oh, look, someone peed in the floor."

He said, "It wasn't me."

The children said, "It was her."

"No, I didn't," I said.

"Yes, you did," they chanted.

The teacher said, "It's all right, don't worry. Why don't we take a bathroom break while I clean it up?"

While in the bathroom, the girls were mocking me about peeing on the floor.

I said to them, "No, I did not. If I did, then why are my clothes not wet?"

One girl said, "She is right, her dress is dry."

But the other girls did not want to believe it.

I was so small that I could not open and close the heavy steel door of the bathroom. I had to wait until someone opened it to get in or out. We were all lined up along the wall, waiting to get a drink of water. Just as that big door was closing, my fingers got caught in the crack of the door. I asked one of the girls to open the door for me so I could get my fingers out. She would not. She did not want to get out of line. I could not get anyone to open the door. I had to wait until someone else went inside to open the door. By this time, I was crying, and the teacher asked what happened. Momma and Dad were not at all happy when they found out and saw my broken finger. I didn't trust anyone at school after that. I just played by myself and learned.

Maxine age 6

I had a close friend who lived right next door. We played hopscotch and jump rope. We made chains, belts, bracelets, and necklaces with clover. We were not allowed to walk to each other's houses alone. We had to walk on the road and over the bridge. When we would get to visit, the older children would take up to each other's houses. There were several children of all ages. It seemed that each one of us had found a new friend. There were many card games and fun for everyone at one house or another. There were several boys of all ages, and they sure could get into something to do all the time. One day, they were rolling around in an old tire. One boy would curl up inside the tire while the other one would hold it up then give the tire a push to get it going. They did that and counted the minutes to see who could keep the tire going the longest. The two of us girls wanted to do that too. It looked like so much fun. The boys laughed so hard. They finally gave us a turn, and that was all it took. When the tire fell over, and it did right away after they gave it a push, that was rough and hurt, so that was enough for us.

One morning, the older girls were helping Mom in the kitchen. She almost passed out. On the way to the bedroom to lay down, she collapsed. My dad caught her. He asked her if she had eaten, and she had not. He scolded her for not eating. She knew that she had to eat. One of the girls brought her some crackers, and after she ate a few, she felt better. I remember her saying something about her iron maybe low. My mother was always vitamin B deficient, which caused her to have anemia at times. I heard Daddy ask Momma if she thought she might be pregnant, and she told him no and that she was sure of it.

Chapter 35

Soon after, we moved. It was a small house at the edge of a cotton field. I went to Paragould School for a while.

I hated it there at that school. There was a boy in the third grade who was three times larger than me. I could not play at recess, and after school, when we had to wait on our school bus to come, he chased me. The teacher who was on duty said, "Oh, he just wants to play." Well, no, he didn't. He wanted to hurt me and did every day. I tried to stay hidden from him, but he always found me and wanted to hurt me; he even said it.

One day, I was playing with some classmates, and he tried to hurt one of the girls. Then he saw me. He said he wanted to hurt me instead. I could not believe that he really did until he started toward me, and I knew that he was not playing. I ran. I could not get away from him; he was everywhere. I screamed and cried, "Help! Help!" No one would help me. They were all afraid of him. I found my brother Nathaniel on the playground that his class played on.

He scolded me. "What are you doing here? You will get in trouble!"

I was crying and explained to him that the mean boy was coming toward us.

Now Nathaniel was not much bigger than me, even though he was two years older. He stood up to the boy. There was some pushing and shoving between them, and Nathaniel walked off to go find the teacher. She called the boy in to her room and told him to leave me alone. He was mad. It did not help, no matter how much she talked to him. Every day, if I could not stay hidden from him, he chased me.

One day after school, he chased me and would not let me catch my bus. I was instructed by my parents to go immediately and find my older sisters and stay with them until the bus came, and that was what I always did. But on this particular day, he would not let me, and I ran from him and tried to find a way to get to the bus. I screamed and cried for help. Then he caught me and pushed me hard. I fell forward with both knees sliding on the gravel. Blood was everywhere, and I could hardly walk. I made it to the duty teacher's room while he was behind me. She did not even scold him.

She just said in a really soft, gentle voice, "Now, now, we must not play that way."

I cried and told her, "Why didn't you make him leave me alone?"

She said in the same voice, "I will talk to him again." Then she turned to him and said in the same voice, "She is little. You are a lot bigger than her. You have to be more careful when you are playing with children who are smaller than you."

I cried to her, "I keep telling you that he is not playing. He said he wanted to hurt me."

She said, "Oh, I can't believe that."

When she had finished cleaning and nursing my cuts and scrapes, the teacher took him right to his bus stop and let me go to mine. My brother Gerald had come to find me. Dona had sent him to look for me. When he did not return right away, she decided to look as well. When we got to the bus stop, the bus was there, and Dona was gone.

I asked Lona where she was, and Lona scolded me and said, "She went to look for you! Where were you? You know to come straight to the bus stop!"

I tried to explain to her, but it did me little good. The bus would not wait. Dona was left behind. Dad had to go back to get her.

My mother was terribly upset when she saw my knees. She and my dad was more understanding than Lona and went to the school the next day and had a talk with that teacher. That boy never bothered me again. In fact, he treated other children that way, and that duty teacher just did not know how to manage him. I never even saw that boy at school anymore.

After school when we got off the bus, the older children would change into work clothes and walk out of the yard into the cotton field, where my mother and father would already be picking. Nathaniel and I wanted to pick very badly. After much begging, my mother found us a large lard bucket to put our cotton in and let us go to the field. When we got the bucket full, she would empty it into her sack, then we would start again. After a few days of that, she told us we graduated and gave us a pillowcase with a strap on it, just like a real pick sack, and we could not wait to fill it up. Before the end of the season, she had found time to make us a sack out of pieces left over from worn-out sacks that could no longer be used except for patching holes on the other sacks. We loved it and picked if everyone else did. Isn't it funny how young children love to help?

Chapter 36

My grandfather, Lindsey, came to visit often. He brought lots of vegetables from his garden. He also brought vegetables to store in our cellar. This had been Grandfather's house before he let us move in here.

My grandfather was very patient with us, answering our questions and explaining all about everything. He had turnips, squash, potatoes, pumpkins, cabbage stored in the cellar, and I am sure that is not all, but that is all that I can remember.

We went to visit him regularly too. He and my grandmother lived at this time in a tent. Amazing. It was set up just like a house. Grandpa had told Dad that he decided to live in the tent. He could set it up until it was just like a house, just as clean and comfortable. The way he was always moving around to work, it was better for them. Too many times they had a hard time finding a decent house that didn't need fixing up before you could live in them.

The tent had a wooden floor and bedrooms, living room, kitchen. It had a wooden cookstove and heat stove in the living room and was very cozy and roomy. Grandma seemed happy enough with it. She had plenty of room for all her furniture in the living and bedrooms. Her kitchen was roomy too. She had plenty of room for her cupboards, freezer, table, and stove. She even had shelves across the wall by the back door. She had the shelves with jars of food that she had canned. We could see the pride and enjoyment of her accomplishments on her face. Mom was like that too.

Every house we were at, the women would have pride in showing off their canned food. The men would take pride in the meat hanging in the smokehouse. People worked with contentment and peace. They found joy in just being able to have a place to raise what they needed to provide for their families and maybe sell or trade something to help buy the other things they needed. Jobs were scarce and money was short from what jobs a person could find. Most families were packing up and moving to the northern states to work in factories. The ones that hadn't gone yet were handing onto all they could to keep from having to go too.

My grandmother always had something for us in the freezer that she had made or picked. One of our favorite treats were the wild muscadines Grandfather had picked and she had frozen for us. She always had ice cream too. Grandma gave us milk from her milk cow and fresh butter on hot biscuits that she made from the sweet cream she skimmed of the milk. Sometimes, she had fried peach pies for us. She had a peach tree in her backyard. She canned and froze the peaches. The frozen peaches were used for her pies, and the canned peaches were for eating right out of the jar. They were delicious. She also had a plum tree. She froze some of them and some she made plum preserves that we ate with those buttered biscuits.

Her milk cow's name was Betsy. We loved to tease that old cow. We had cousins who lived right down the road. They would come up and play. The boys would take off their shirts and wave it at Betsy, and she would charge them like a bull. They would run and jump over the fence to safety. Grandmother would scold them; she was afraid it would ruin Betsy's milk. They would keep on until Grandpa would come out and make the cousins go home. The boys had knocked a board off the fence running from Betsy and jumping over the fence. Grandpa made them fix it. He and Dad watched to make sure they did it right. After the fence was fixed, Grandpa sent the cousins home. They were being too rowdy. He had trouble with them every time they came, wanting to use Betsy for a bull and pretending they were bullfighters.

If you ever wanted to get Grandpa upset at you, then don't get Grandma upset. When you messed with her cow or turkeys, you did just that. After a time or two of telling us to leave them alone, she would then go to Dad and Grandpa. they would get upset over two things. One was disobeying Grandma and getting her upset, and two was interrupting their conversation and causing her to make them go and take care of it all.

And we wouldn't play outside long after that because the turkeys would chase us. Grandma said the cousins made her turkeys mean. When we would get off the porch, they would run us back. If we went out the back door, they chased us around the house and right up on the front porch after us. We didn't attempt to go out many times because of those turkeys. Grandpa said that it was a shame since he loved those boys and liked to be around them, but they were just too rambunctious.

Grandma made us Kool-Aid and Kool-Aid popsicles that she made in metal ice trays. She always had plenty of those.

We enjoyed just sitting around in the living room with the grown-ups and listening to them talk. Especially there in that tent. It was always toasty warm and very pleasant. I really do believe that the warmth must have come from Grandma and Grandpa themselves.

They talked about politics, the shape the war had left our country in, and about the past.

Grandfather Lindsey's family came from Scotland. There, they were dukes, earls, lords, bishops, kings, and queens. They were married to children or siblings of the kings and queens from England, Spain, Australia, Whales, Scotland, and France. Here in America, they became just regular people like the rest of us. Although through their riches and influence, they helped build this great nation. They built cities and set up governments. Now we are all subjects to that government that our ancestors sacrificed to build. Did you ever stop to wonder how your ancestors got here and wherever did they come from? If you think about it, they had to have money to venture off on that great voyage when they traveled over the great seas and to be able to survive until they were established with housing and work. The people who made that great voyage either had money, knew someone with money to help them, or worked long and hard to try to save enough. If they couldn't do that, then they came over as endured servants of someone who was able to pay their way and work for them for a certain period of time until their debt was paid off. Often the masters would not want to let them go, and if they did, they might keep the spouse or a child to work for them for another period before releasing the whole debt. Life was not easy for many people after they came to America. It was a chance to be free, to have a life and own land they never had in their own countries. Many of them had to let one of the family members go on ahead until they were settled and could get the money to send for the rest of the family.

One of the stories they told us was about our dad. He had one blue eye and one hazel eye. It was almost like Maw's eyes, but it was browner. Her eyes were brown with a lot of amber starbursts inside the brown ring. We had asked why Dad's eyes were like that, and they told us. Grandpa and all his sons were going to sign up to join the army. They wanted to do their duty to their country. On the way riding in the wagon, Dad saw something in the road. The wagon wheel had almost hit it, and when he saw what it was, it frightened him. It was a dynamite cap. If the wheel had hit it, they would have blown up. Dad yelled for them to stop the wagon, and he jumped off to get it out of the road, so it would not be a danger to someone else. Grandpa and all the boys hollered for him to stop, but he did not understand why, so he picked it up, and it blew up as he threw it, and a fragment came back and hit him in the eye. He lost his sight in that eye.

He did not get to go into the army because he was blind in that eye. He was always disappointed because he didn't get to go to fight for his country. He said it was a man's duty. He had a picture of his brothers during the war.

Chapter 37

S oon after that, we moved to Bradford, Arkansas, where I finished my first grade of school. This is my first-grade school picture. I loved going to school there, and I loved my teacher, Mrs. Cox. She took me in like a little lost sheep and made me feel welcomed and treasured. I loved most of the schoolchildren too. They all played together, and I was welcomed.

We lived in a house in the country. We had a lot of company out there. After meals, everyone would go outside and play horseshoes or softball. Some of the parents played, and some of them sat on the porch and visited.

We didn't get to live there long before we moved into Bradford. We still lived there when Grandpa Lindsey passed away. He had a coronary artery disease. After the funeral, everyone gathered at our house. All of Dad's siblings were there with their families. Our house was full; the funeral home was crowded as well.

Some of the women were helping Mom and the girls in the kitchen. The men were all in the living room talking. The children were running everywhere as usual. Uncle Edward was playing with some of the children when we noticed that some of his fingers were missing from one of his hands. He told us that they got shot off during the war. The soldiers were in a skirmish, and he went to wipe the sweat off his forehead and noticed that they were gone. He said they were so busy trying to beat the enemy and keeping from being killed that he hadn't even noticed.

It wasn't long after this that we moved into a big two-story house. This house belonged to a distant relative, Mr. Mitts. He and his family had moved up north and bought a farm. They had not planned to go back, so we could live there. He had furniture, and

Mrs. Mitts had a lot of canned foods upstairs. He told Mom and Dad that they didn't know when they would be back, so if there was anything that we wanted, just help ourselves to it. Mom would not even go upstairs. She told Dad that it wouldn't be right. They had worked hard for that stuff, and she knew that Mrs. Mitts and those girls worked hard to put that food up, and she wasn't going to touch it. She said that they might need it; people never know what is going to happen. This house sat close to a church. And there was just an empty lot in between us. The empty lot became Mom's garden spot. The church became our home church. The pastors of that church had been our pastor before at a church in Ingleside. He also had been friends to our family all my life. He was Jackie's father, Brother George. There were many people in that church that we knew and had been friends with. This made the move to a new place less strange.

Jackie's brother, Cloyce, was always begging Mom to make him a cake. He liked the yellow layer cake with the hard chocolate icing. I think he could eat a whole one all by himself. Every time their family came to our house to eat, Mom would cook him one.

Jackie did not try to cling to me as he did when we were younger. Even though I got a spanking for biting him, I think it did some good. He treated me more like a litter sister, just like the way Nathaniel did. He never tried to hold onto my arm or hold me by the hand or any of that. When we would be in competition together at different functions in Sunday school or at church socials, he didn't even mind that I would beat him. I think, like my brother most of the time, he just let me win. We are in a much better relationship now.

We liked living there a lot. Gerald, Nathaniel, and I walked to our schools only a few blocks away. Mom had a huge garden spot; she took the whole lot up between our yard and the churchyard. We had a field out behind the barn for corn. Mom had enough chickens to provide the family with eggs, and Dad had a couple of rabbit hutches with tame rabbits.

We raised corn to eat and can, but Dad let the ears of corn dry in the field for chicken feed, hominy, and cornmeal. Dad had a grinder set up on a cook table in the kitchen that he would use to grind the corn into chops for the chicken feed and then he would grind some finer ones for cornmeal as the younger children watched him. We would argue over who would be the first to use the grinder. After a while, it became our job to grind chicken feed and cornmeal.

Chapter 38

Oh, my goodness, it was too early to get up. Climbing out of bed, rubbing my sleep eyes, stretching, and yawning, I asked "Why do I we have to get up? "I heard my Joyce and Nathaniel protesting as well.

Mother walked out as Lona and Dona took her place, helping us dress and get ready for our morning. Dad stepped in and encouraged us to eat a little breakfast, informing us that we were all getting ready for a trip.

We really didn't understand where it was. Walnut Grove, Dad had said. But we did know who was there. Dad's family lived at Walnut Grove. We were excited to know that we were going to get to play with our cousins.

Ferry that we rode on at Oil trough

"Oh, Dad, will we get to ride on the ferry?"

"That's the only way to get across the river," he replied.

It would be different this time. Last time we crossed was in a wagon drawn by a team of horses. When the horses got a little rowdy, we were afraid. This time, we would be in a car. The car would not get rowdy and act up that way.

As we grew closer, there it was, the ferry at Oil Trough. We pulled closer to the water. The ferry was coming back from the other side, taking cars over and bringing them back. The first time I remember riding on it was when we still had the team of mules and rode in the wagon. I remember being afraid that the mules would get scared and take off the end right into the river. Dad parked the car on the big ferry and got out to talk to the man who was running it. Dad knew everyone, I thought.

Soon, we arrived. There were several houses in a row down the road: one row on the right and another down the road. Right, left, right, left. Dad would tell us who lived in each one. They were all his relatives. The first house lived Dad's oldest sister, Aunt Ruthie. She wasn't home. She had several children, but we didn't get to play with them that day. The second house was on the opposite side of the road and down several hundred feet. This was Aunt Ruby's house. They were home. Her children, the twin girls, were sick. They couldn't go outside. Linda had well gotten over her cold or whatever it was, but Brenda had not and was coughing her head off. Well, on we went down the road to visit Uncle Wilbur and his family. He has several children just like us, and they were all about the same age as we were. Aunt Ruby and her family came later to visit also. We had a bunch of children playing outside, and the older children congregated on the screen porch.

Uncle Wilbur and his wife, Aunt Effie, were glad to see us and so were their children. The subject of Aunt Ruby's sick girls came up. Uncle Wilbur was saying that they were never going to get well as long as she kept letting them run around outside, playing in the damp and cold. He said that most of the time, they didn't even have anything on their arms or heads. He went on to say that he had told her about it more than one, and if you ask him, that child had the whooping cough. He was glad his kids had the shots, so they wouldn't get it. But Aunt Ruby wouldn't get hers the shots; she was afraid too. She had heard so many bad things about the shots.

"I warned her," he had said.

Dad had replied, "Yes, I am going to do what I can for mine, to keep them healthy. There seems to always be something going around. If you can do something to keep illness down, you're a fool not to."

We later found out it was whooping cough, but we didn't get it from her because we all had the shots. Now Aunt Ruby had to listen to Dad and Uncle Wilbur telling her how wrong she had been for not getting her children the shots. There just wasn't any need for the children going through all that when she could have avoided it by just getting them their shots.

We played outside. It was very chilly. Linda and Brenda didn't even have long sleeves on their arms; the rest of us had a jacket or sweater on. Brenda took spells coughing violently without stopping. Her face would get bloodred. We offered to go in the house and play with her if she would go in, but she didn't want to.

We were called in to eat. Some of us took our plates with sandwiches and chips to the screened porch to eat. The porch was partly enclosed, then there were several windows with a small part screened letting the room be warmed by the sunshine. With large plush chairs and a couple of couches, it was a perfect place to gather on what had been the beginning of a damp dreary day. Then the sun appeared with its bright warm beams warming the day on. The girls sat talking about how we would make a playhouse out there, and we played there when it was cold outside then, a teenager, came in the door from outside. He let us know right away that it was his porch. He stayed out there most of the time. He often slipped out there to smoke. *Wow!* What in the world! Didn't he think he would get caught and get in trouble? No, he didn't, and he didn't care. *Oh my gosh*, he acted so tough that he scared us off his porch just by talking like that.

Chapter 39

Mom got word that Maw was in the hospital with pneumonia. Maw had been living with a lady who was bedfast and taking care of her. She often gave this kind of care when someone needed her to care for their sick loved ones. But now she was sick and was coming to our house when she was released from the hospital.

Dad helped Mom fix a bed up for her in the dining room, where she could still be around the family as she rested in bed. Dad took care of her just like Mom. She was awfully sick. He would fix her soup and feed it to her. He had taken a chair and cut a hole in the middle of it to set a bed pot into for a bedside pot. She couldn't walk to the toilet. Like most people, our toilet was an outside toilet. He would help her up to use the toilet and help her back in the bed. Then he emptied the pot and washed it before returning it to the chair. He would place a chair upside down in the bed and pad it with quilts, so it would be comfortable for her; it helped her lay at an incline, so she could be able to talk to us and watch us move around.

Soon, she was able to sit up by herself and even walk a little. It took weeks before she was able to get completely out of bed. She was worried and so was Mom and Dad because she was so weak for so long. Mom and Dad would sit by her bedside and try to comfort and encourage her. She was cheered up when Dad came home from the post office. Mom received a letter from Aunt Lola, her half sister. Aunt Lola and Elizabeth lived in Oklahoma. They were coming to visit. They would be coming through and then going onto north to the fruit and vegetable harvest. It had been a long time since we had seen them. Everyone was excited. Mom, Dad, Maw, and all the children sat in the living room and waited for them to come. Mom had gotten everyone up early and rushed us around to have our breakfast and get all the house cleaned up before they got here.

They arrived and brought with them boxes of gifts. A hairbrush and mirror set were for Lona and Dona; they were shiny silver with elegant floral engravings. I don't remember what everyone else got because when Aunt Elizabeth gave me my doll that she had brought me, I was too excited to notice anything else. She said that I was her special girl, and she said that when she knew it was a dancing doll, she thought that she had to buy it for me. It had reminded her of me. It was just my size and had slots on the hands and feet to slip my hands and feet into, so we could dance around. She showed me how to do it and whirled around the floor, dancing and laughing with the doll and me.

She kept hugging me and laughing. "You got it," she would say, "a natural-born dancer. I knew you were. That is what you will be when you grow up, a dancer. Probably ballet."

"What is ballet?" I asked.

She tried to explain it to me. "Oh! how I wish I was close so I could teach you. We would have the most fun."

I don't think that I ever got to see her again.

Dad had come home from the post office with a letter in his hand. He did not look very happy. He read it to Mom, and it said that Mr. Mitts' daughter was getting married and wanted to move back to Arkansas. He had given her the house. He also wanted to know if there were any furnishings upstairs left. He wanted to let her know, so she would know what she needed to bring with her. We all were sad. This meant moving again.

Chapter 40

It was right after Aunt Elizabeth's visit and the letter that we packed up and headed north ourselves. We were on our way to Indiana to work in the vegetable harvest. Mom didn't want to go either, but being that Dad was without a job, we would soon be without a house to live in. It looked like they did not have a choice.

The truck was loaded, and we were waiting for the evening to come. Dad thought he could make better time if he drove at night. The children would be asleep; he would have less distractions from the little ones and less bathroom stops, plus there would be less traffic too.

After the sunset, we loaded up in the truck. This time, Maw did not go with us. It was just Dad and Mom in the cab of the truck along with Loyd, Joyce, and me. Lona, Dona, Gerald, and this time Nathaniel were in the back. As usual, they packed only the bare necessities. And left room in the middle of it all for the four children to set on a bench that Dad had put there for them to sit on. Off we went.

While driving along, Dad had said, "I sure do hope that the harvest is good, so we can make some money. If it is and we can afford it at all, I am going to buy me a bathtub, so I can stretch out in that tub when I bathe. I am tired of being all squinched up in this washtub trying to take a bath."

Mom had laughed and remarked how nice that would be.

The next thing that I remember was stopping at that little country store, where we always stopped at for a break and bologna for sandwiches. A little farther down the road, there was a place where we always stopped. Dad pulled a mattress off the truck and laid on it for a little rest. Mom took a quilt and spread it on the ground for a picnic, with our bologna sandwiches, chips, and soda pops that we got from the store. There were just enough fried pies left for each of us that Mom had packed for the trip.

The next time we would stop would be when we got there, to that long row of rooms that people used for their homes during the harvest.

When we arrived, it was already dark. One of the disadvantages of arriving after dark was there was no electricity. They unloaded just what we needed for the night from the truck. Everyone was really tired from the trip and each of us were trying to get beds off the truck and putting them up for the night. We only had three rooms. One room was extra long; it was used for the living room, dining room, and kitchen combined. Two were for bedrooms. Mom, Dad, and the two little ones slept in the small room from the kitchen. The other bedroom was a little larger; it had room for two beds. One bed was small. It was for Gerald and Nathaniel. And the other was a large bed the three girls shared.

The next morning, Dad took Mom's two-burner gas stove off the truck and set it up. Mom unloaded her kitchen supplies and cooking vessels and made breakfast. Lona unloaded boxes from the truck while Dad and Gerald got the rest of the furniture. Dona was getting the children dressed and fed them their breakfast. After breakfast, Dad took off to the grounds of the factory to see the man that they had come to work for during the harvest. He later arrived and assured Mom and the girls that everything was good and that they all would be able to start to work the next day.

After all was unpacked in our temporary house, they all began to look up and down the row of rooms to see who we knew had come. There were several families that we knew, some distant relatives from Virginia. Everyone was glad to reunite with each other. A girl down the row volunteered to babysit. Her family was always there too, and she had finally gotten old enough to babysit her younger siblings. Mary also had a sister who babysat for some of the other children in the camp. Mom needed a babysitter for Joyce and Loyd, but she felt like Gerald could watch Nathaniel and me. Well, that worked out fine; Gerald and the babysitter were soon to develop a crush on each other. The babysitter's name was Mary. She had several siblings to watch. When Gerald would go to see her, we would all play together. There were more children in their family living in the temporary houses just like us. We all got along well together.

Mom and Dad often visited with the neighbors next door. William and Martha. They were from Virginia, where they lived on a tobacco plantation. Every time we met them in Indiana, they were asking us to visit them in Virginia. They didn't own the plantation, but the lady's grandparents did. They always came to work in the harvest when their work on the farm was slow. They were trying to save enough money to buy their own land and build a home on it.

Their son, Will, was the same age as Nathaniel. He was an only child, so he was happy to have someone to play with. There was a wagon down at our rooms that came from the loading dock. It was a large steel flatbed wagon, large enough to hold several children. When we got tired of that, we played king of the mountain until one boy got pushed off and hurt his head. We had to leave it alone for a while after that. We loaded it up, and one of the larger children would pull the others around. We did not have much to play with besides the wagon. We had old maid cards, a checkerboard, and softball; that was about it.

Nathaniel helped me build a playhouse. Behind the house there was a small yard, but it was larger than what we had in the front of the house. Mom did not want me to play back there unless Nathaniel or someone was at home because of the railroad track that ran nearby. There was also a small amount of water standing between the tracks and the house. Momma and Daddy thought that it was running off from the showers and toilets or the factory. It smelled bad at times, especially when it was hot. There were cattails growing in the water. Nathaniel would take me to pick the cattails, so I could use them in my playhouse. He made me a table out of two boards and some cement blocks. He brought me some cement blocks for chairs. We looked around and found broken dishes for the table and ten cans, small tuna and Vienna sausage cans, for pots and skillets. We used the cattails for decorations and food. I used a wash pan from the house for my dishpan. I had to make sure it was back in the house before they all came home for lunch and supper.

Nathaniel played with me a lot. There were weeping willow trees growing near the water. At first, we cleaned out under the tree and put our playhouse there. Then it was hot, the misquotes were too bad to play in there, and Momma was a little concerned about that. She did not want us to catch something from the misquotes. When she was around eight years of age, she had typhoid fever and almost died. She lost all her hair and could not walk for a long time. Again, when she was twelve, she fell off a horse and broke her back. While she was down trying to heal from that, she caught malaria; she almost did not make it through this. The way she described to us her reason for being so careful with us, we listened well. We did not ever want to get that sick.

It was left up to us to fix our lunch. Mom could not leave the factory to make it for us. We knew how to open a can of something and cook it on the stove. On this day, as I opened a can of creamed-style corn, I took the lid off, and there was a large worm laying right there on top of the corn. I set it aside, so Mom could see when she got home. She did not work on the corn line. Dad did, but he worked father up the line where he took the corn off the truck. Mom worked on the green bean line, and both Lona and Dona worked on the regular corn line, the whole kernel corn. They all were going to report this.

Mom was visiting next door, and while sipping coffee, Mom had mentioned that I had a birthday in a few days.

"Oh, wow! Are you going to have a party for her?"

Mom explained that she just didn't have the time to do much; she was just planning on dinner then cake.

"Please let me do it, I would love to. I can bake her a cake."

"Oh, no," mom replied. "I am so grateful to you for wanting to do this. I wouldn't want to impose on you."

Martha was so excited. "No, not at all. It could make me so happy."

Mom finally agreed to all but the cake. She explained to Martha how it was a tradition that all the girls baked their own cake when they turned seven years old. Being that there are seven ingredients in a cake if they baked it on their seventh birthday, they could remember easier how to bake one.

Maxine age 7

"Well, what a good ideal." Martha replied, "Just leave the rest to me. And don't worry, it will be so much fun."

It didn't take me long to remember the seven ingredients in that cake and how to mix it up.

"Now let's get your bowls and mixer out and set them right here. Next, we will put all of our ingredients out side by side," Mom instructed. She stepped back to see if I remembered what they were.

"Okay, here it is," I said to Mom, "flour, sugar, baking powder, salt, butter, eggs, and vanilla flavoring."

"Well, that is mighty fine, you did remember." She was pleased. "Now let us see if you know what to do first."

I picked up the butter and carefully measured it out, one-third cup. I put it into the bowl, then I measured the sugar, one cup, and poured it into the bowl. Next, I mixed it with the handheld mixer and rolled the handle round and round until the butter and sugar were mixed and until it was creamy as icing. Then came the eggs; they were mixed the same way. Then the tablespoon of vanilla. Mixing it more. Mom had told us if we wanted a light fluffy cake, to mix it extra well. She sipped her tea and watched as I took the other bowl and measured the dry ingredients into it—one cup flour, one tablespoon baking powder, and a dash of salt—and I mixed it together with a spoon.

"That's great," she assured me.

Before she had time to say anything else, I picked up the bowl of dry ingredients and poured a small amount into the wet ingredients' bowl and started mixing again and again, a small amount at a time. Mixing it well in between would make the cake lighter.

She didn't have to say anything; she was pleased with me that I had remembered. I had watched her enough that it was easy for me. She had lit the burner and warmed the iron Dutch oven. Just warm enough for it to melt a small amount of shorting. Then she showed me how to rub it all over the pan. Then she sprinkled it with flour to keep the cake from sticking to it. She set the burner just right on a low setting and put the lid on the pan. We did not have an oven. Most of the people in the camp only brought enough to "batch" by, as they would call it. So they usually had a two-burner stove that used kerosene to run it. Martha had been there to watch. She thought this was just the most amazing experience for her to witness. We all set and sipped tea and talked while the cake was baking. Soon, the cake was done, and Mom let it cool a while then turned and placed a plate onto the top pan then turned it upside down. The cake slid right out onto a plate.

"Look at that, it is just perfect," Mom said, pleased as she could be.

Martha laughed and clapped her hands. "That's my girl!" She couldn't stop giggling as she gave me the biggest hug; she squeezed me until I could hardly breathe.

The party was great. All the children from the camp came. There were so many children. The wagon had been pulled out from the hiding place by some of the children. Someone went in and told the adults, but they decided to give us another chance to play with it without getting too rough and causing an accident. Everything went along just fine for a while and then someone pushed Nathaniel too hard that he stumbled backward, falling, hitting his head in the hub of the wheel just like Will had done. Nathaniel was passed out, laying on the ground with his head bleeding. Some of us started screaming. I ran in to get Mom and Dad. Some of the children thought he was dead; they were scared so they went back home.

William and Dad were examining Nathaniel and discovered that he needed stiches. Martha asked if I could stay with her, William, and Will while they took Nathaniel to the hospital. She didn't want me to feel so bad since Nathaniel and I were close to each other. She did everything that she could to keep me from crying and worrying. It wasn't long that I fell asleep there in her kitchen booth while she read to Will and me.

It was just a few days after the party that Will and Martha left and returned home. The tomato harvest was nearly over, and several of the families had already left. The families that did stay were hoping for a chance to fill in for those who had left, so we stayed behind as long as we could. Dad was hoping to make that extra money, so he could get his bathtub. Here at the camp, right in the middle was a long row of showers as well as basins and even clothes washers for the women to share. He was getting a little used to bathing without having to be cramped up in that washtub.

Chapter 41

Work was slowing down, and it gave us a chance to go to town. Everyone was looking for something to spend a little of their money on. While Dad took the truck to get it serviced for the trip home, Mom took us to the park. It was right in the square, so as soon as Lona and Dona had a chance to shop, they came and watched us while Mom went. She had run across Gerald at the variety store and told him to run down to the service station and tell Dad to stop by and pick her up, so she wouldn't have to carry her packages. Dad and she had measured the feet of us younger children, so she would know what size shoes to get for us. We mostly went barefoot during the summer; our feet had grown, and now we needed new shoes. They came and while Dad picked Mom up at the variety store, he found himself that bathtub. He was so proud of it.

They took their time packing up and loading the truck. Daddy hung his bathtub upon the side of the sideboard along with the washtub, the foot tub, and the dishpan, which were hung on the other side. Everything was packed little at a time, except the stove. Mom wanted to be sure we had a good breakfast before we left for the road. She made biscuits that she cooked in the Dutch oven with gravy and scrambled eggs. She made a lot of eggs, so she could make sandwiches for the road. This time, instead of the homemade pies, she had picked up snacks at the store. Dad was helping clean up for the rest of the loading of the truck while Lona and Dona got the little ones ready for the trip. Momma also made a jug of tea and water for the trip just as she always did, trying to think of everything.

After a little discussion, Dad and Mom agreed that they would just go by the folks in Virginia. As soon as they got back home, they would have to hit the cotton fields. Work never stops. They deserved this. The only protest with Mom was the way we had to travel. Why, we looked like a bunch of hillbillies. That truck filled up like that, things hanging off the side. It was bad enough to be filled up the way it was with kids, heads sticking out everywhere.

"My goodness, woman," Dad retorted. "Just look around at these other people up and down this road."

Sure, enough Joyce and me looked for a good while. Yep, there's one and there.

"Look, Momma, there goes another."

It was an awfully long trip. But I think Loyd, Joyce, and I slept most of the time. Momma held Loyd in her lap, and Joyce and I sat between her and Dad. When we were awake, we colored, looked at books, and played with load. Sometimes, I would beg to ride in the back of the truck with the rest. Mom didn't want me to; she was too worried about it, but after much begging and the older girls promising to keep a careful eye on me, she gave in. I loved watching the two older girls no matter what they did. I wanted to act like them. They stood up on the bench and looked out over the top of all the furniture. They took turns holding me up, so I could look out too. I watched them and tried to imitate them as the wind blew their hair all over, and they tossed their heads to shake it out of their face. They were afraid the wind would damage their hair, so they dug some headscarves out of a box. The wind was so strong that they had to hold the scarves on their heads, so they just sat down and read stories to me.

I woke up as I heard Dad and Mom remarking to each other how beautiful the countryside was. As far as you can see, there are tobacco fields. Between the plants, trees, and grass, there were all different colors of green.

"Is this it?" I asked.

"Not yet," replied Dad. "We still have a piece to go."

I fell asleep and, again, woke up to them talking to each other.

"I think this might be it," informed Dad.

We had been following a white fence for a little bit before we came upon a long driveway with the same white fence all the way down. The whole place was fenced in with it. There was a large two-story house with several other smaller houses around. They were all white trimmed in green. So were all the barns, sheds, and all the buildings used for drying and storing the tobacco.

The grandparents lived in a house along with Martha's mother and father. She and William along with some of her siblings and a couple hired hands each lived in the rest of the houses. Her grandfather and grandmother still worked the farm along with the rest. Though her grandma and mother spent some time at the house doing the household duties and keeping the book worked up, we enjoyed our rest, and Mom and Dad enjoyed their visit. William took Dad out to the fields with him to show him around and explained to him the methods they used in growing and harvesting the tobacco. Dad was pleased with what he had learned. He told Mom, "I wouldn't mind growing some of this tobacco for myself, for my own use, but I don't think we could manage a farm."

We were on our way on the road again. After we had traveled quite a way, there was a car pulling a trailer with sideboards; it was loaded down like our truck with bathtub and washtub hanging on the side. The driver fell asleep and was on our side of the road. Dad tried to miss the car; he swerved the truck over to the side of the road. *Bang, bang, rattle, rattle.* The noise woke the other driver up. After the automobiles came to a stop, they ran to each other to see if anyone was hurt. The man was sure sorry. Dad helped him gather up what they had lost and drove on down the road. There was so much going on from their conversation about that poor man and his family.

Loyd was crying, and Dad was being nervous by it all that he didn't even notice he had lost his bathtub. We pulled over at a station to take a little break. Dad let us all get out to stretch our legs and get a soda.

While he was paying for them, a lady standing nearby spoke up. "Aren't you the man that was driving that pickup back at the scene of that accident?'

"Yes, ma'am, that was me," Dad replied.

"Well, it's just too bad that you lost your bathtub. If you go back and get it, I think you might still be able to straighten it up and use it…if you can get back there before someone picks it up."

Dad almost got choked on his soda. "Well, uh, thank you, ma'am. Yes, I will go back and get it. I was so shook up I didn't think to check. Thanks again, ma'am. You have a nice day." He almost ran out the door, trying to get to the truck so he could go back and check on his bathtub.

When we got back, there it was. It was a little bent, but he said he could fix it, and it would be just fine. If it leaks, he could fix that too. But he found Momma's dishpan had been dropped too, and it couldn't be fixed; he would buy her another one.

"That's all right," she told him. "That thing has been dragged all over the country, banged up already. I could use a new one anyway."

Then they had a good laugh about it all. Momma said that she never would forget how he looked when that lady told him about his bathtub. Every now and again, they would start laughing about it all over again.

Chapter 42

Dad had gotten a letter from Mr. Mitts before we left Indiana. His daughter had decided that she didn't want to move away from the family, so we could stay in the house as long as we wanted. Everyone was happy about that. I had been to three different schools in my first grade, and I didn't want to start a new one this year. School had just started. Gerald, Nathaniel, and I got back there just in time. Dad and the girls got back in time to pick cotton.

After the cotton season was over, Lona found a job in Newport taking care of an elderly lady while her daughter worked during the day. Dona found a job at the corner drugstore as a waitress and grill cook. They both rode the Greyhound bus to work and back every day. Dad worked in the logwoods or anything he could find to do.

During the winter, all of us little children got the measles, and soon after, the mumps went around. I didn't get the mumps as bad as the rest, but the ones who had them on both sides sure did look awful. We couldn't eat. Fortunately, everyone didn't come down all at once, so there was a grown-up left to care for the rest as they came down sick.

We got to finish all our school year at the same school. We were in the same classroom with all the children we had been with the last year and made new friends up and down the block. As it was with most young children our age, we were playing with friends in one house or another, and school was all there was to life and our church family, of course.

Chapter 43

The next spring, Dad had found a man with a tractor to work up the garden spot for Momma. He plowed it and disc harrowed it up too. Dad went over it with our garden plow until the dirt had the large dirt clots out of it. He made the rows for her to plant. He whistled and sang as he worked. While he worked at his job, she planted the garden little at a time. When school was out in the afternoon, Gerald, Nathaniel, and I helped her. On the weekend, everyone helped. They always tried to have an early garden and a late one. Dad always said we could have two gardens if we had the second one planted by July 3. Mom liked to plant the things that grew better early first and the things that grew better later on second. Unless her crop of a certain vegetable had not produced as much as she needed for what she wanted to can. Of course, she would plant that again. Now there were some things such as sweet potatoes that had longer growing and producing periods. They could only be planted once. Potatoes were always planted twice. It took a lot of canned goods to feed all of us until next garden time produced.

The first thing in the garden to eat were the lettuce, radish, and green onions. They sowed the lettuce seeds and radish seeds and planted the onions in the onion bed that Momma had made. She raked up the dirt into a wide area and shaped it up. Raking the dirt as smooth as she could. There was an area of dirt about a foot wide and six feet long. She made two—one for the white and one for the yellow. Then she showed us how to make a row across the bed; she wanted it straight, so she gave us a flat stick to measure it across. We laid the stick across the bed and took our finger and drew a line across the bed. She showed us how far apart to make our lines. Then we poked a hole into the dirt in the dirt line and put the onion into the hole and covered it up. Down the bed we went, with yellow and white sets as close as we could get them together. Goodness, we really got tired before we got all the sets planted. We set on the ground for a while, reaching over the bed until our backs ached, then we kneeled on our knees. When our knees got tired, red, and hurt, we sat again. On down the row. I planted the white onions in my onion bed, and Nathaniel planted the yellow ones in his onion bed. We looked every day to see if we could see any little green stems coming out of the ground. The best way to eat the green onions made from these bulbs were to cut them up, mix them all together with the lettuce and radishes, then pour hot bacon grease over them. Everyone I knew ate this. Nathaniel was through before I did and went to help Momma plant the onion plants. I didn't care if I was left there setting on the ground by myself because I did not like to plant those onion sets. They not only made your back hurt, and it seemed like it took forever to get the rows planted. These sets looked like stems of grass, sticking them in the ground and pulling the dirt up around each of them, so they will stand up straight. The green stems dried up and looked dead before they started growing back again. The onion sets were for the larger onions for cooking and slicing for sandwiches. The cabbage plants were planted differently from the onion sets; we had to space them father apart, so they would have room to grow. We dug a hole with the hoe and put a little fertilizer in and pouted a little water in then put in the plant and pulled the dirt up around the plant, so it would not fall over. Momma did not want the plants to lean to the side. She liked all her rows perfectly straight and plants evenly spaced and standing tall as they grew.

After we had all the plants planted, the whole family helped to plant the potatoes. Dad brought in a large sack of Irish potatoes. Dad always called them Irish potatoes. They were not actually Irish potatoes because they were red. Irish potatoes are white. However, Mom liked the red potatoes better because not only were they better for either frying or mashing and tasted better in her soup, stew, and other dishes, but they are healthier for us.

We all gathered around and worked the table for the potatoes to be planted. Dad, Lona, and Dona cut the eye off the potatoes with a good hunk of potato for planting, and Mom took the rest of the potatoes and washed it and sliced it up for frying for supper. After we got a pan of them cut up, Dad went to the garden to start planting. Nathaniel and I were eager to help. We followed right behind him.

He set down the pan, and he said, "Well, if you want to help, you have to do it just right. I am going to show you what to do. Now don't forget." He dropped a piece of potato with an eye on it in the dirt. "Now place it in here like this. Now be sure you put the eye looking up. Take your feet and step like this in between the potatoes. I must do one step because my feet are larger."

We picked up a handful and walked up the row.

He said as he walked away, "You plant there and I will start up here."

So we picked up a piece of potato and placed it in the row with the eye sticking up, looking at us, until we caught up to where Dad was. Then he would walk on up ahead and give us some more space to plant. When we got through with the row, he started back down, covering the potatoes up. If we had one laid in the row wrong, he would pick it up and change it after he showed us what we did wrong. He tried to show us how to cover up the plants with our feet as we went down the row.

"Save a lot of time this way," he said. "Just walk along and scoot the dirt over the plant with your shoe as you walk along."

So we tried but our feet were too small to pull much dirt over. He showed us how to pull the dirt over with a garden hoe. We liked to do the work. Sure, we got tired, but we wouldn't give up and quit.

Now they always planted potatoes earlier in the spring too. So we would have some new potatoes with our English peas. Then it wasn't long until the English peas came on, ready to pick shell and be canned. Nathaniel and I carried empty jars from the barn and washed them. We kept the firewood sawed with a crosscut saw and split, so we could keep the fire going under the washtub to wash and rinse the jars in. Mom wanted the water to be as hot as we could handle it, especially for rinsing. We used a long ladle to stick down in the jar and dip it in the hot rinse water. Mom was hesitant about letting us do this; she was afraid we would get burned. We begged to. We just always wanted to be able to do whatever they were doing.

When we got all the vegetables planted, we planted some watermelon and cantaloupe. We had waited to see if we would have room for a few plants. Dad loved to grow these too, but we had to wait this time to see if we had room. And we did. We were so happy. I jumped up and down and clapped my hands. So all were in the ground, and we were waiting for things to start growing. We used a push garden plow to plow the garden while we were waiting. Mom was afraid for me to use the garden hoe, but she let Nathaniel use it in places that she could not get the garden plow.

Summer wore on, and we had a lot of time to play with the neighbors. There were a few up and down the street in both directions.

Ruby, one of our friends, had a birthday party. We went to the party. She had balloons and party whistles. We had games that everyone could play. Children of all ages were there. When it was time to open her presents, Nathaniel and I gave her hair bands and hair bows. She loved them. One of the presents that I would never forget came from one of the boys across the street. It was a huge box wrapped in pretty paper. She was so excited; she quickly tore it open to find another box wrapped in pretty paper. She unwrapped several boxes all wrapped in beautiful paper until she got to a tiny box. By this time, she wanted to throw it all in the trash, but her older sister wouldn't let her. So she opened the box and found fifteen cents. She said thank you and put the money in her bank. One of the boys said, "Is that all?" We laughed. Ruby was pleased because fifteen cents would buy her a soda, a candy bar, and several pieces of bubble gum. We had a lot of fun.

I spent much of my summer playing with Joyce and Loyd while Nathaniel took his BB gun and went to the woods with his friends. They would take their fishing poles and go fishing. I wanted to hang along, but Momma always said no. I was used to Nathaniel always being there for me, so this was quite different. Since Joyce hung after me like I had always with Nathaniel, I was glad to play with her. Loyd was learning to walk and was all over the house. Momma had barricades over each doorway to keep him from getting out. We had moved the kitchen table to the back porch; it was so much cooler. It was all screened in, but Momma had to keep the screen door locked to keep Loyd from trying to push it open when she went to the garden to work. Joyce and I tried to keep him busy. We would walk him and try to get him to walk to us, and he was learning very well.

Chapter 44

We had been back to Ingleside for a church service and to visit with relatives. On the way back home, just as we drove over the levy at Newport, Dad turned to drive down behind the golf course and high school, as we always did, and we ran right into a storm. The sky turned all black, and it was only a little after 5:00 p.m. The wind and rain came down hard. We were all so frightened. Mom asked Dad if he thought he needed to pull over. He told her no, that we would be safer if we kept driving and tried to drive out of it. The lightning came popping and crackling, and all the little children cried. The older children tried to quiet us down, so Daddy wouldn't be bothered by all the screaming and crying. Daddy started singing "This Old House." Mom had been praying. She stopped and started smiling at Daddy trying to get us to sing with him. The noise in the car from all of us little ones singing out of tune and laughing at Daddy's motions as he sang was so loud that we didn't hear the storm.

Trees were uprooted, large trees that were hundreds of years old. The highline wires were popping and sparking as they blew in the wind.

When Daddy got to the part about of the song, "Ain't got time to oil the hinges," Momma said, "Yep, those shutters are probably really flapping right now." We all laughed. We thought Daddy was talking about our house, and when Momma said that, we really thought he was.

Daddy said, "If it is storming like this at home, that ole house might not be standing."

We did not take him seriously. He had been so much fun. As we drove along the road, I can't be sure how long it took us to drive through the storm. It was dark outside and hard to see all the damage, but sometimes, from the lights from the car, we could see the big trees that had fallen.

Dad and Mom did not say too much except that they thought it had been a tornado that went through the town. They thought that it had been a large one. When we got home, the house was still standing. We asked Dad if the wind had torn the shingles off, and he said no, he didn't think so. We were glad that the house was still looking solid and didn't let in any rain. They just chuckled at it and put us to bed.

When we woke the next morning, Dad had already been out to access the damage. The house was fine everywhere, but there was a large black walnut tree down in the backyard. Daddy and Gerald began trimming it up and saving to best wood for firewood. Momma checked on some of the neighbors close by, and they told her about the storm that had come through while we were gone. Tornadoes were no stranger to the residents of Arkansas. And we did live in the deadly tornado valley. Right through the center of Arkansas. The tornados usually followed along Interstate 30 and US highway 67/167. This was a big year for the storms.

Chapter 45

The garden was producing very well. Lona, Dona, and Mom were busy canning. They kept Nathaniel and I busy sawing logs and splitting the wood for the fire from the tree that the storm had left us.

Mom had said, "I hate to see that ole tree go even though I did not like the mess that it made from those black walnuts. It was nice for shade."

Dad and Gerald trimmed it up and left the best wood for firewood for the cookstove. They didn't have time to saw it up in logs or split them before they left for work. Lona and Dona had started that task. After Nathaniel and I had begged to help out, they messed with us for a while and saw we could do it all right then left it to us. This was one job that we liked part of the time and hated the rest of the time.

Mom used a lot of wood for canning and the washtubs of water that she used to wash jars. Oh, yes, that was another job. We would carry the jars from the barn and bring them up to the house. If they were very dusty, we had to rinse them off in the water that was in the foot tub beside the fire. We had to keep clean water in that tub too, then we had to check them for cracks or chips around the top. If it had a chip, even a teeny, tiny one, it would not seal right, and her food would be wasted. We then put them into the water to wash. We had to carry all of our water from the pump in the backyard then wash more. We would go inside to see how many jars they needed. We had to leave them in the hot rinse water until she was ready for them. Then some of us would take a dishpan of jars to her, and she or one of the older girls would put them into a pan of hot water on the stove. Before they would accept the jars, they would inspect them. They would look them over good. If they see even the tiniest spot or if they felt a rough spot when they rubbed their finger around the top, they would send it back. Nathaniel and I learned to do the inspecting ourselves before we ever let our jars go to them. We didn't want them to think that we could not do the job. Jars and lids had to be kept in boiling water for a certain canning process. If Nathaniel and I got behind on the wood or jars, then Lona or Dona or both would come and help us. They would get up early and pick the vegetables and get them ready for canning in the morning before the process would begin.

Sometimes, Nathaniel and I would get to help shred the cabbage and stuff the jars for sauerkraut. We also liked to help with the green beans. We could snap off the ends and break them into the proper length then put them into the jars. There were quite a few things that we could help with at our age. We did enjoy most of the jobs, and most of it did not seem like work at all. Mom always wanted to have at least one thousand quarts of food canned up for our family to make it to the next garden season. She canned vegetable soup and chicken and dumplings. She canned rabbit and squirrel and whatever she thought we would eat. We liked rabbit and squirrel dumplings too. She kept a cold pack canner and a pressure cooker both going, and we had to be careful in the kitchen around her jars and help her keep count of the pops from the lid sealing, so she would know that they were all sealed. She did not want any of them to fail her.

We—Lona, Dona, Nathaniel, and I—were all outside, and Joyce and Loyd were taking a nap, then we heard a boom. We ran inside. As we entered the back porch, we heard Momma from the kitchen, "Well, my word. How on earth did that happen? What a mess I have now." When she saw us, she started laughing. There were pinto beans all over the kitchen, walls, ceiling, cupboards, floor, and everywhere.

"Oh, be careful, don't slip down," she said. "How on earth will I ever get all those beans off the ceiling?"

We were so glad to see that she wasn't hurt. Needless to say, it was all soon cleaned up, and the canning came to a halt for the day.

Chapter 46

Maxine age eight

School started and I was going into third grade. Nathaniel was going into the fourth grade. It was exciting to see our classmates and begin our new school adventure for the year. A lot of different things were to happen during this year that were unbeknownst to us at that time. We didn't need to know; we just needed to bask in the moment of each day as we got used to the school year. Nathaniel, being a grade ahead of me, always kept me filled in on what was to be learned in the next year for me. As he showed me the different things, I learned them right then. I wanted to be a show-off when the time came. Nathaniel always had the best of grades, and I was learning from the very best.

Lona had begun to date a boy who lived in the country, and Dona had started dating his brother. She had finally gotten over Richard, her old boyfriend that we did not like. They were mad about each other and thought they were in love with each other. Richard's family thought Dona wasn't good enough for him being from a poor family across the field, *that* family who lived in that old house and had all those kids and didn't have anything.

Dona had met Richard at the drugstore café in Newport where she worked. They had gotten to know each other and started dating. But finally broke up because of so much pressure from his family. He went away somewhere; she was heartbroken for a long while. Now she met Odell, Dale's brother. She was getting over Richard fast. It wasn't long before Lona and Dale got married. We hated to see her leave the house and go with him; we missed her so much. But since they both worked in Newport and came through Bradford just a few blocks from our house, they stopped by very often. Odell was in the air force and would see Dona when he could come home. One day, he came in and told her that he was going to be transferred to Massachusetts and would not be able to see her very often. He wanted her to marry him, so she could go with him, so she did. What on earth would we do without both Lona and Dona?

It was almost Christmas, and Odell and Dona did not have to leave until after the New Year. Momma was very happy and so were the rest of us, but little did the younger children know that a surprise awaited. For us. Momma got sick and had to go to the hospital for a couple of days. Maw came to stay with us to help, and both of the girls were there when Daddy brought Momma home. What was she carrying in that blanket bundled up in her arms? Dad had her by the elbow, watching every step she made. And when we got in, she laid down on the bed—the one they had moved into the living room for her—and everyone was gathered around her, excited to see what it was she had. Then they started handing her around for everyone to hold and pulled Nathaniel and I up close. A couple of them grabbed Loyd and Joyce and held them near. "What?" their expressions seemed to ask.

"Look, here she is, your baby sister. Her name is Caroline Jean."
Wow, were we ever surprised.

Joyce reached out and wiggled her fingers, wanting to hold her. She thought she was a big baby doll.

Chapter 47

Everything had quieted down in our household, but it wasn't the same without the girls. One day, Dad had come home and told Mom that he just could not find a steady job here, and he had spoken with a farmer that he worked for before at Ingleside. The farmer told him that he had some work for him, so up we went and packed up and moved back to Ingleside. There were a lot of things that happened in the next few months. We finished our year of school out in Newport; I was at the Newport Elementary School—a very large two-story building close to downtown Newport. Nathaniel had to go to another building; it was over by the high school.

Momma had been painting the kitchen. She used kerosene to clean her brush. She had a fresh glass setting on the cupboard. Daddy came into the room just as he saw Joyce set the glass down.

He said, "What did you have in that glass?"

Mom told him, "Just as I thought."

He said, "Joyce thought it was water, I reckon. She just drink out of it."

"Oh no," she said. "Lord have mercy. I never thought about that."

They grabbed her and started trying to get her to vomit and worrying over her. Then she went unconscious. I don't know how they got word out to everyone in just a short time, but the preacher and his wife came over and the neighbors and another family. They were all laying hands on her and praying for her, and Momma fainted; she was still fragile from having Caroline. This time, she has already turned forty-two years old and was just worn out from having children and trying to help provide for them. The neighbor boy, Charles, had come down with his parents. He was a really good friend of Nathaniel's, and I thought that that meant mine too. We were all worried about Joyce but tried to keep ourselves busy outside, so we wouldn't be a bother.

The two boys decided to go crawdad hunting down at the slough. It had just rained, so they ought to be crawling around. They said I could go with them, so I wouldn't have to be alone. All three of us got a large coffee can out of the dump behind our house and went to the slough. Naturally, I thought that I had to outdo them, so I was trying hard to get the most. Then they decided to go to the other side of the slough and told me to stay there. I had so many crawdads that they were crawling right back out of my can. They were so big that when they stood up, their front pinchers hung over the top of the can, and they were tipping over the top right into the water.

I reached down in the water to pull them back about, and Charles said, "I wouldn't do that. Maybe there's a snake down under the water, and it might bite you."

"No, you are just saying that to keep me from having the most."

Nathaniel said, "No, he isn't either."

So I reached down again, and oh my gosh…I felt something stick my finger. I thought, surely that it was a crawdad sticking me with the front of its pinchers. The boys saw and jumped up and ran across the slough to me. I was in shock as I looked at my finger and saw two little red bloody marks just about a half or three-quarters of an inch apart.

"No, it's not!" I said. "It was a crawdad."

"No," they both chimed in at the same time.

"That looks like a snake. You better go and tell Mom and Dad," Nathaniel said.

Charles agreed, "Yep, you better hurry too."

So I dropped my can. They had told me before that if I got bit by a snake that I would have only around thirty minutes at the most, depending on which kind of snake it was that bit you and until the poison gets you. Just a few minutes for some. Don't get scared because if you do, the poison goes through your body faster. So I just hurried home. I started through the back door. I heard them praying. I did not want to disturb them; we had been taught to have respect and not do a thing to disturb people. Sometimes, distractions can disturb a person's frame of mind and the spirit can't work. I turned quietly and went back out onto the back step and sat. I began to feel very tired as I sat there worried when it hit me…

So I prayed, "Dear God, if this is my time to die, then I am not afraid. But please forgive me of everything that I have every done wrong, so I can go to heaven with you."

Here came Nathaniel and Charles.

"How are you feeling?" they asked. "Are you feeling sick?"

"Just a little," I replied. "I am mostly tired."

"Did you tell anyone?" they asked.

"No," I said. "I didn't want to interrupt and keep the spirit from taking care of Joyce."

They both sat down on the step with me, one on each side, and tried to console me. They kept telling me that they didn't really think it was a snake, so not to worry. They both put their arms around my shoulders and told me stories and jokes until I felt better. We did not even tell the adults about it. They were good to me; they often would take me squirrel hunting if Momma said that I could. Sometimes, she would not let me go. She thought I was acting too much like a tomboy. Sometimes, the boys even let me check their rabbit snares.

Chapter 48

One day, it was raining hard. The boys did not want me to follow them; I tried to anyway. Off down the dirt lane I went in the rain. As the hard raindrops hit the dirt and sand, the dirt popped back up. Mixed with the water, the splashes looked like little soldiers popping up. I was so fascinated by that, that I just got carried away until I felt like I was right in a battle with them. I talked to them. I saw generals and captains, lieutenants, sergeants leading their troops. We ran, and we stopped to look for the enemy. The rain stopped, and my soldiers disappeared. I called for them to come back, but they didn't. I slowly walked back down the lane, back toward the house. As I walked across the bridge, I stopped to see how much water was flowing under it. We often played in that water. Sometimes, I would sit on the bridge and hang my feet over the edge. Most of the time, the water was so clear that you could see all the way to the bottom, but this time, as I looked in it, it looked awfully muddy. But it was moving. I watched. Then I saw it… Why, someone had thrown an old tire into the water, but wait! It looked a little smaller that a regular tire. Maybe it was of one of the farmers' tractors or some more of their equipment.

Well, I am going to see if I can get it out, I said to myself.

So I looked around until I found a nice round stick, about twice as big as a broom handle and about as long. I stuck it into the tire and thought I could get ahold of it right under the rim and pull it out. But ewe! What in the world! It's a snake, or it felt slimy because it has been under the water and had sediment on it. So I put my stick in again, and the snake stuck its big head straight up, and I had the creepiest feeling that I have ever had. I threw my stick and ran as hard as I could to the house and told Momma.

"Now you know why I don't want you playing in that water," she said.

Later the boys went to the yard. They had seen me and evidently had been watching me the whole time.

When I told them, they said, "Yes, we know, we have seen snakes in there before. We can't play in that water anymore."

They didn't laugh at me though. They never laughed at me or made fun of me. They had seen me playing soldiers with the raindrops, and I felt embarrassed.

But they said, "It's okay. We do that too."

I was fine with that. Through all our childhood, Nathaniel and I were remarkably close, and all his friends always treated me like a little sister.

Charles had an older sister; she was a lot older than him. He didn't think of her as a sister though, but he knew that she once lived in their house. She still had a room at their house. Her childhood toys were still there. He played with some of them. He made me a playhouse under a big, shaded tree in their backyard and asked his mom if he could bring some of his sister's things out for me to play with. She was a very sweet woman, and she would smile when he asked her and watch him as he brought them out and helped me with the playhouse. Finally, I think he must have brought the whole setup of her room out. I had a whole housekeeping setup. A stove, refrigerator, sink, cabinets, table and chairs, dolls and cradles, even an ironing board and an iron. I felt like I was in paradise and spent many hours playing under that shaded tree in that playhouse. If it was going to rain, we would drag the whole setup into their back porch and leave it until everything was all dried up then take it back out again.

Chapter 49

We waited for the school bus at Maudelene's store; there were several children there waiting every Morning. Maudelene had a son, Gary. He was my age. He would bring me an apple or orange every morning. At school, he bought me an orange from a big tub of oranges the school passed around to the classrooms. If a child had a nickel, they could buy one. He never talked to me. He would just hand me the apple or orange and smile. I would smile back, and he would take off to be with his friends. He had a cousin who came down to catch the bus with us. His name was Dale Turner. He grew up to be a DJ at the radio station in Newport. I don't know what happened to Gary, but Charles became an airplane pilot.

Momma did not have a spot for very much of a garden there to raise the food she needed to can for us. She just had a few chickens in an old chicken house. Things had not worked out so well as far as Dad's job was going, and after the crops were planted, he didn't have any work. So he went to find a job at a factory in Newport. That did not last long either. He had left to go find a job somewhere, but he did not come back. It wasn't time for Mom's garden to produce yet, and we had no food. Every day, we went out around the slough and along the road, around the fields, to look for any kind of poke salad or other greens to mix with then make a meal. Sometimes, we could hardly find anything. Momma's hens gave us a few eggs, but it wasn't enough to feed all of us.

Daddy was gone all the rest of the spring and all summer. Lona and Dale had seen us a few times, and Maw would come up and spend a few days when she could. She was working for one of the farmers that lived in the area, caring for his wife and baby boy. His wife had muscular dystrophy, and after the birth of their son, she never regained her health. She was bedfast and could not care for herself or the baby.

It was a terribly lonely summer. Our hearts ached for those who our hearts longed to be reunited with. Momma had such a hard time being way out in the country without a car or any way to get around. Then again, here she was with a baby who was only a few months old, a toddler of age two and a half, a five-year-old, nine-year-old, and eleven-year-olds. Of course, there was Gerald, sixteen years of age. He had become so restless that Mom could barely handle him. He was gone, running around with friends most of the time. One of his friends had a car, and the boys just ran around the countryside all the time, keeping the roads hot in that car. Momma was always trying to talk to him, but he did not listen to her. Some of the boys worked just enough to get money for gas and dating and what fun they wanted to have, but that was all. Mom didn't know where he was most of the time, and it had been a while since he had heard from Dad.

I heard her and Maw talking about dad.

"The least he could do is write to you and try to send you a little money along to help you. There just isn't any reason for him doing you like this," Maw said. "You don't need to take him back this time."

It set my mind to wondering; he had been gone a few times before that, I could recall. *Why?* I thought. I was old enough to know it wasn't a good thing.

Then I heard Maw say, "My goodness, Ador, he leaves you alone with all the children knowing that you don't have any way to get around, no way to provide for you and all these children. He can't seem to keep a job. Just one after another."

My ears perked up. Well, this was something that I never thought about before, but it was beginning to ring a bell. My word, look at how many times we moved around.

Mom answered, "Well, I know. He had a hard time controlling that mouth too. That did cause him some trouble sometime."

"Now, Ador, don't start holding up for him. You know if he can't find a job, where he can put you and those children, out in the field doing all the work for him. While he takes off to town messing around and don't come back until you all got it all done when he gets home. Then he don't hold down a job. He can't get along with anyone long enough to work for long," Maw said to Mom. Her tone sounded as if she was getting angry at Mom for trying to take Dad's side.

Mom answered in an irritated voice, "Now, Mom, he has always treated you right, hasn't he? Didn't he take care of you while you were so sick? He will be back. I am sure he will."

Maw almost jumped out of her chair. She was getting angry. "That don't make up one bit for how he has done by you and all these children. And you know it."

Mom was about to cry, and Maw apologized to her; she told her she was just worried about her and the children. I sat on the steps, just thinking, trying to sort it all out in my mind, trying to justify my dad but couldn't understand why he didn't write Mom a letter.

We started to school in Newport. Every day on the way on the bus home, we watched all the cars pass the bus and disappear into those brown dusty clouds.

Now on this day, it was very irritating for the bus driver. "You would think those idiots would have a little respect and realize that dust is not only choking us up, but I can't see a thing when they do that," he remarked.

Then came a car, very fast and passing the bus.

The bus driver said, "Now I wonder what fire he is going to."

The car pulled over a little way in front of the bus, and the man got out and started flagging the bus to stop. When the bus stopped, the man began to greet the bus driver, but the bus driver was yelling at him and calling him names for driving like that and stirring up all that dust, maybe causing him to wreck the bus with all us children in there. As the man began to apologize, Nathaniel and I recognized his voice. Nathaniel was seated a few seats in front of me. He looked back at me, and we jumped up and headed for the front of the bus. The bus driver stopped us at the door but was still listening as Odell was trying to explain how they had been gone for a long time and was just trying to get ahead of the bus, so they could flag him to stop, so they could get us off. It was not an uncommon thing for people to stop buses to get their children off. The bus driver calmed down and let us go and told Odell to be more careful and to not drive that fast with us children in the car.

We were so glad to see them. Odell had gotten vacation time, and they came home. Dona was so glad to be home. She didn't even get mad at Joyce and me for getting to her trunk and ruining her pretty dresses. As she was going through her trunk after Momma told on us, she just said, "Well, I probably won't ever be able to wear them again anyway." Then she told us the good news, she would be expecting a baby next spring.

They were disappointed to find what shape Mom was in with Dad gone. Not at her but at Dad. They talked her into trying to sign up for some assistance. She was so embarrassed to, but she gave in; she saw there was no choice. They went down and paid Maudelene what Momma owed her, though she didn't want them to. But she knew it was a matter of pride for them and Mom. Momma had sent Gerald down to help do whatever he could do to help out with their farm and at the store, but he didn't do much; he was too interested in Maudelene's daughter, Maggie, who was sweet to him to. She was supposed to be tending to the store. They didn't work out very well, so Gerald had to stop going down there, distracting her. Mom was embarrassed and angry with him. Nathaniel went and helped her with her wood then feeding the animals and whatever he could, and Mom traded her eggs and chicken for groceries, so she wouldn't owe so much. Dona and Odell told Mom to pack her things, and they would get her moved back to Bradford before they left to go back to Massachusetts.

Lona and Dona set out right away to find a house for Momma back in Bradford. It wasn't long before they found one and had us moved back. It was a large two-story house right out of town, about two miles away, but we could still walk to town to buy what we needed. But most of the time, Lona would come once a week to take Momma to town if she needed to. The rolling store came by there too. Lona and Dale came right by the house every day on their way home from work. Lona was expecting a baby too. Hers would be born after the first of the New Year. Oh, wow, what a delight. Momma was going to be a grandma, and we were going to be aunts and uncles.

Chapter 50

We got by all right there at the new home, but it was hard on Mom to walk that far to Bradford, so she started inquiring to see if she could find a place closer to town. In the meantime, Daddy found us, and there he showed up out of the blue. He was there a while and gone again. He didn't have a job, so Momma told him to leave. She couldn't afford to lose what help she was getting because he came back. If he made her lose it, then she might not be able to get it back. If he got a job and stayed with it, he could come back.

After a few months, we moved to town just a couple of blocks from everything. The downtown was right across the street from the school. Daddy still hadn't got in touch with Mom that he had a job, and he hadn't sent her any money. Dona and Odell had come back again, and they along with Lona and Dale and Maw, of course, all got together and talked Mom into getting a divorce. For quite a while, Momma knew why he had stayed gone for so long. Aunt Virgie, Maw's sister-in-law, told Maw that Daddy had been going with her niece, her sister had told her. They had both gotten together and told her niece that he was married, had a house full of children, but she would not believe that it was the same man. I never will forget how I cried when Mom told the rest of us children that Dad would never be coming home again. Of course, Loyd and Caroline never knew him enough to really know who he was. Nathaniel cried too, but Joyce wasn't old enough to understand.

A few months later, after the divorce, Dad tried to come see us. He came to the house, but Mom made him stay in the car. It just so happened that Lona and Dale were there that day. Momma told Dad that the lawyer told her if he brought child support, to let him visit;

but if he didn't, then don't. So he said that he did, but he wanted us to go home with him, and he would go buy us clothes and whatever we needed and then bring her back some money when he brought us back. She told him no. She thought he was trying to trick her, and if she let us go, then he would not bring us back. He left and did not leave her any money. That was the last time I saw my dad until I grew up.

We had a rough life. Mom had a rough life trying to raise us. She worked in the cotton fields, babysat, worked in cafés, took in washings, ironings, sewed for people, cooked for people, and did their hair. Anything she could do that was close enough to home that she wouldn't have to leave us for long so she could walk to get there and back home. Anything that she could so she could provide for us. I remember my mother would be up at night mending and falling asleep in her chair. Maybe she didn't get but two or three hours sleep before she started all over again. When she wasn't trying to work for someone else, she had a lot to do at home. We learned to help her, and by the time we were teenagers, we could cook, wash, iron, and keep the house like grown women. Nathaniel worked at whatever he could do. He would help cut wood, split wood, haul hay, and care for other people's lawns. By fourteen years old, I was already helping to care for elderly ladies and babysitting. Nathaniel and I were picking cotton when we could, even though we had to get out of school. In the spring, we picked strawberries.

Maw had moved to Bradford also and lived right next to us. Dona and Odell had moved to Blytheville; he was stationed at the air base there. We were glad to have them back near home. Lona and Dale had moved to Illinois to take jobs in the Del Monte factories. Gerald had gotten so wild and would not listen to Mom. He was trying to sign up to go into the military but could not find a branch to take him at the age of sixteen, so as soon as he turned seventeen, Mom signed for him. He went to the marine recruiting office and brought them out to the house to show Mom. She cried but she thought it was best for him.

Sometimes in the summer, Lona would come and get me, and I went home with her to babysit for her and some of her friends. I made more money that way than I could with what I could do at home. I could help Momma by making school clothes for the other children too. Nathaniel would go out and stay with Dale and Odell's parents; they had another boy a year older than Nathaniel. They hauled hay all summer for different other farmers close by. After school started and cotton-picking season came along, sometimes, Dona would come and get me. I would be out of school for two or three days and go with her. I babysat for her and her friends while they picked cotton. It helped them make a little money for clothes and things for their children, and I made more money babysitting than I could picking cotton. Sometimes, she would come on Friday and bring me back Tuesday. That way the men were off work and went with their wives to pick cotton, and it made them extra money to help them get caught up on a bill or pay something off. Servicemen did not make very much money.

Even though we had been out of school for picking cotton and babysitting, Nathaniel and I managed to make almost all *As* on our report cards. Momma was strict with us about everything, it seemed. She was so afraid that people would look down on the family because she was a divorced woman with a house full of children. Divorced women were looked down upon in her day. We were always careful about our actions and the way we kept up our home. We always had our clothes clean and ironed, our hair kept up; we also wouldn't slouch or drag our feet. Our Ma was always onto us about things too. Sit up straight, hold your shoulders back and your chin up, don't walk around looking at the ground. We were like, "Give us a break," though we wouldn't dare say that to either of them. We would have been slapped cross-eyed. We did not want to get either one of them on our bad side. If we did something that we weren't supposed to do, we would get a switching. Once you got a switch used on you, then you didn't have to get it for a long time since you did everything right. Things had sure gotten to be different since Mom and Dad got a divorce. It was a hard life, but we always had a home for longer than a few months to a year. We always had clothes, and we never went hungry.

I feel bad for the children that were too small to know their dad and to remember a childhood like I cherish. They only had harder times and no memories of a dad at all. They have no memory of a family working and playing together, sharing the love of a whole family gathered in the living room at night, laughing and talking, singing, and listening to the stories. Mom was unhealthy, but she tried to keep it to herself. She was so busy working and just trying to keep our household up that she felt that she had no time to take for herself, for a few moments of much needed rest or just to recollect her thoughts. She had little time for us. She was often cranky and short-tempered, which seemed to distance us from the softness and kindness that we were accustomed to. Little did we know of her pain and hurt that she endured from her health as well as the divorce. Though she tried to hide the bitterness, we could feel it by the way she talked about our dad when his name would be mentioned. Maw was no help. She was right there to encourage such feelings and sometimes to even get them stirred up. Essom had died not many years after Pa passed away, leaving the two to cling to each other.

Dad tried to write to us, but the man at the post office told Mom to hold the letter up, and if she couldn't see a check in it, that he would put it in the dead letter box. This was a box for mail that had not been received, and after a while, if no one claimed it, it was destroyed. The lawyer had told Momma to not let Dad see us if he did not pay child support. We halfway wanted to believe that not accepting the letter was an excuse to keep him away, to punish him. Later we learned that she was so hurt that she could not handle her emotions when it came to him.

The last time Dad had gone away and stayed so long, he had taken up with another woman. She was much younger. In fact, she was the same age as Lona. To remember the condition we were living in at the time and to think about him finding someone else was too much for her. Effie was her name; she did not know that Dad was married. Aunt Virgie, Maw's sister-in-law, told Effie's mother. Effie's mother was Virgie's sister. When the two told Effie about him, she went to him and confronted him about it, and he denied that he was the same man who was married with a house full of children. Later they told Momma the story. We never got to visit with our cousins either because Dad was living among his siblings at the time all this was going on. Mom was bitter against them. She never got to learn that some of them were caught in the middle and did not approve of what he did or had much to do with him from then on. And so life kept on going on and on.

We can't always control what happens to us. For some people, they cannot always handle life, so I guess it is up to those who are born survivors to lift them up and try to give them the nourishment of love and understanding they need to survive.

Maybe it was all for the best. Later when I met my husband, he had been raised up the same way. It gave us stamina to try to do better for our family. My husband and I have been together sixty-two years. We didn't do everything perfect along the way. I am sure our children can vouch for that. But we still have a home for our children, grandchildren, and great-grandchildren. And they have their own memories of all our lives together.

About the Author

Maxine was raised in a small farming community where everyone knew each other and many were family of some degree. As the daughter of a sharecropper, she grew up like the rest of the children in her community, in a life of poverty. This was the time of the post–World War II era. The economy was in bad shape, but most people were survivors.

She was taught by her parents and grandmother, who greatly influenced the lives of her and her seven siblings, that you are never to use the word "can't," as in "I can't do this or that." If a person tries hard enough, they can find a way to do whatever it is that they are trying to do. People can't because they won't; they won't try to find a way to get whatever done. This always seemed to prove itself to be true. This is one of the main keys to survival. Believe in God and believe in yourself. Remember that "through Jesus all things are possible." This has been passed on to the generations of her family.

After living in different states and traveling around to different places, her husband of fifty-five years and herself have settled on a small farm in Arkansas. They have raised three children and enjoyed much time with their eight grandchildren and twenty great-grand-children. They both have played a very active role in most of their lives in church and school. They both love spending time with family and friends, gardening and travel. Much of the inspiration she gets for the articles that she has written for papers and church have come while gardening.